Gladys Peeples

Alan R. Benton

Jim Crawford

Asbury Lenox

John Wesley Hardt

John Croft

Melcia Peeples Harrell

Wayne C. Olson

Cecil Peeples

A Twentieth Century Giant

Cecil Peeples

A Twentieth Century Giant

The story of Cecil Peeples and his years at
Lon Morris College in Jacksonville, Texas

By

Gladys Peeples
Jim Crawford
Wayne C. Odom
Walter L. Harris
John Wesley Hardt
John Croft
Don Benton
Asbury Lennox

Edited by John Wesley Hardt

Published by
UMR Communications, Inc., Dallas, Texas

Design and typesetting by
The Wordwright
Lillian Sills

ISBN 0–9669363–0–2

Cecil Edward Peeples

Born
August 5, 1902

Died
January 20, 1993

President of Lon Morris College
June 1935 – June 1973

Active Retirement
June 1973 – January 1993

Cecil and Gladys Peeples
1973

Dedicated to Eddy Clark Scurlock

"Lon Morris College's Man of the Century"

Cecil Peeples

Courtesy of Jack and Laura Lee Blanton

Eddy Clark Scurlock

Table of Contents

List of Illustrations

Acknowledgment
of
Personal Support

Photographs were provided by Gladys Peeples, Walter Harris, John Croft, Susan Slater Edenborough, John Wesley Hardt, and Lon Morris College. Helen Musick found many pictures, particularly of the emerging new campus.

Belle Albritton provided dates from board records, and produced many pages of photocopy work for reference. Ruth Alexander contributed her memories of Cecil Peeples' travels with students, as well as of Zula and Arch Pearson. Annie Laurie Phillips shared her reminiscences of the 1930s and 1940s. Ed Kiely gave vivid descriptions of Bearcat basketball during the World War II years and the O.P. Adams era. Virgil Matthews assisted with the chapter on developing and retaining a faculty; and Frances Whiteside provided information about her mother, Frances Beall Harris, for that chapter.

Selections from the writings of Cecil Peeples were provided by Gladys Peeples, John Croft, and John Wesley Hardt. The college songs were provided by Gladys Peeples, with corrections, and were typeset by Elbert Marshall, in consultation with Jane Marshall.

Frank Thornton provided liaison with Lon Morris College administration and staff.

John Croft helped with meticulous proofreading, and made many useful suggestions during the editing process.

Gladys Peeples, Nelda Peeples Darrell, and Gerri Peeples Weddle gave their encouragement and support throughout the process of planning and producing the book.

Countless numbers of Lon Morris College graduates and friends offered their encouragement.

Acknowledgment
of
Financial Support

With grateful appreciation for the financial support
that made possible the publication of this book

John W. Croft

Texas Methodist Foundation

United Methodist Foundation of the Texas Conference

Fair Foundation

Scurlock Foundation

Introduction

As Isaac Alexander was the driving force that shaped the character and life of Alexander Collegiate Institute in the nineteenth century, so, in the providence of God, Lon Morris College in the twentieth century was shaped and formed by Cecil Peeples. Also, just as thousands of persons were inspired and encouraged when their lives were touched in some way by either the man or the institution, the legendary story of Cecil Peeples may reach into other lives in the next century and for generations yet to come.

Here is the story of how this book came to be written. When the final decade of the twentieth century was beginning, the chair of the Lon Morris Board of Trustees was Judge Morris Hassell of Rusk, Texas. Judge Hassell was also a member of the Lakeview Methodist Conference Board of Managers, another East Texas Methodist institution. From the Lakeview Board, he was named to chair a committee charged with producing and publishing a history of Lakeview as it approached the fiftieth anniversary of its beginning. I was invited by the committee to write that history. After several meetings across a number of years, the Lakeview committee was completing its final meeting when Judge Hassell turned to me and said, "Now that you have completed the Lakeview history, will you consider writing the history of Lon Morris College?"

It was only a seed of an idea, and it remained dormant until after the death of Cecil Peeples in January 1993. Then the seed began to grow.

The memorial service for Dr. Peeples was in First United Methodist Church, Jacksonville, Texas. Invited to provide the principal leadership for the service were three Lon Morris alumni: Dr. Asbury Lenox of Houston, Dr. Don Benton of Dallas, and Bishop John Wesley Hardt.

Several months after the service, I invited the other two participants, Dr. Lenox and Dr. Benton, to meet with me to explore how the life of Cecil Peeples might be recorded to include some of the history of Lon Morris College. Many options were considered, and the idea was discussed with Mrs. Gladys Peeples, widow of Cecil Peeples.

After considering a variety of suggestions, I invited a dozen individuals to meet on the campus of Lon Morris College to consider the plan of having different persons write different chapters that would tell the story of Cecil Peeples and Lon Morris College. I presented to the group a suggested outline for the book, which was revised by the action of the group assembled. Writing assignments were accepted by mutual agreement.

Chapter One on family background and early life of Cecil Peeples was written by Gladys Peeples, with the support and assistance of other family members.

The story of the school before the arrival of Cecil Peeples, and other dominant leaders who left a lasting impact, was written by Jim Crawford, an ordained minister and chief financial officer of the Texas Conference. Crawford is a graduate of Lon Morris. He is the son of Nace Crawford, a second career pastor who entered Lon Morris as a student the same year that Peeples became president; and the two became intimate, lifetime friends.

The story of a young president and a bankrupt college was written by the Reverend Wayne Odom, a Jacksonville native who began appearing in Lon Morris drama productions in childhood. Following his student days at Lon Morris, he continued a lifelong, close relationship with Peeples and the college.

A chapter on Peeples' relationships with students was suggested by Asbury Lenox, and was written with the cooperative effort of several participants.

Asbury Lenox assumed leadership for obtaining the financial resources that made this project a realistic possibility.

Multiple chapters were entrusted to Walter L. Harris who, following his Lon Morris student days and further education and career choices, returned to work as business manager under the Peeples administration. After leaving Lon Morris, Harris was associated with the Jacksonville Public Schools, serving several years as superintendent. Following early retirement, he returned to Lon Morris to fill interim responsibilities. With access to school archives and knowledge of many key players in the years of campus expansion, Harris wrote a chapter on developing trustee leadership, and another on the emergence of a new campus. Then, along with longtime academic dean of Lon Morris, Virgil Matthews, and others, Harris put together a section on developing and encouraging the faculty.

Another Jacksonville native and Lon Morris alumnus, John Croft, who became a senior legal counsel for Exxon Corporation, wrote the chapter on the retirement years. He also shared in coordination of the plans, and gave clear, practical and legal counsel for making possible the implementation of this dream.

A final summary chapter describing Peeples as "The Great Encourager" I put together from many sources. Following graduation from Lon Morris, I served several terms as a member of the Lon Morris Board of Trustees, returning to the campus for many speaking invitations, and with my wife, Martha, enjoyed a lifetime personal friendship with Cecil Peeples.

As the plan began to unfold, Croft and Hardt invited Lillian Sills, diaconal minister of the United Methodist Church, an experienced and skilled editor and professional consultant for publishing, to present a proposal for taking the efforts of this team of dedicated individuals and producing a valuable record.

The writing team proposed, under the leadership of Lenox and Crawford, to raise the needed funds to finance the production of the book from longtime generous benefactors of Lon Morris.

Seeing the need for startup funds from his involvement in every phase of the production of this book, John Croft was the first donor to the financial challenge facing the committee. As president of the Texas Methodist Foundation, Tom Locke responded immediately to the opportunity to contribute. Faulk Landrum, another former president of Lon Morris, was eager for the United Methodist Foundation of the Texas Conference to be included as a sponsor. With the long personal relationship of Cecil Peeples and the Fair family, including his years of service on the Board of Directors of the Fair Foundation, Wilton Fair secured the participation of the Fair Foundation. The major support of the Scurlock Foundation was ensured by Jack Blanton, Sr.

Without the generous contributions of these dedicated friends of Lon Morris, this book would never have been produced.

The College agreed to receive the contributions for this purpose with the understanding that when the books were distributed any funds generated would be placed in a permanent endowment fund at Lon Morris to honor the Peeples legacy.

The project became a labor of love in which every participant felt highly honored and privileged to share. Some of the facts and stories will be duplicated in this book. We think this is acceptable and will present multidimensional perspectives of a multidimensional man. Please keep in mind that the person credited with authorship of a particular segment of the book is responsible for that content and the perspectives he or she has contributed.

Recognizing that this book represents only a minuscule report on the influence of the more than half century leadership of Dr. Peeples, this work is submitted with the hope that those who have been inspired or challenged in any way by this story will respond in dedicated and informed service to Christ and His Church, and that other "giants" will follow in an Endless Line of Splendor.

John Wesley Hardt
Bishop In Residence
Perkins School of Theology
Southern Methodist University

November 1998

Chapter One

The Early Years
by
Gladys Peeples

Family Background

Cecil Peeples' paternal grandparents were Alfred H. Peeples, born in 1839, and Celeste Cincinnati Paschall, born June 18, 1843. Alfred H. Peeples and Cincinnati Paschall were married September 16, 1860, in Fulton Tennessee. A family story relates that they eloped. She was said to have climbed from her upstairs window and to have reached the roof of the porch by using a broomstick to bridge the gap. Many years later she was killed in a fire that destroyed her home.

Alfred and Cincinnati had ten children, five boys and five girls. Because I do not know the order of the births, I am listing the names in alphabetical order: Cager, Dave, Don, Newt, Perry Lovick, Agnes (Fry), Alpha (Terrell), Ella (Armstrong), Maggie, and Roxie (Lowe).

It was from Roxie's daughter, Lee Ella Lowe, that I got the above story. Lee Ella was a teacher and she lived in Fulton all her life. We visited with her several times on our way to Owensboro.

***

Cecil Peeples' maternal grandparents were Robert Alexander Kirk (1858-1892) and Mary Ellen Pollock (1855-1938).

Robert Alexander Kirk and Mary Ellen Pollock were

1

married July 25, 1875, in Lawrence County, Tennessee. They moved to Lingleville, Texas, several years later. Their nine children were five boys and four girls: Obe, Robert, Ira, Cain, Laura, Mary and Ona (twins), Abby, and Marvin.

Robert Alexander Kirk was killed in a hunting accident in 1892, leaving Ellen to raise nine children as a single mother. The youngest, Marvin, was born a few months after his father died. Ellen developed a strong feeling of family loyalty among her children, who had a family reunion on her birthday every year until her death at the age of eighty-three. She was also a favorite of her grandchildren and her in-laws. During her last few years she chose to live with Laura, Cecil's mother, possibly because Laura, too, was a widow, with two sons not yet grown.

***

Cecil Peeples' parents, Perry Lovick Peeples and Laura Lou Kirk, were born in Tennessee. In 1875, Perry was born near Fulton on the line between Tennessee and Kentucky. When he was about grown, Perry left Tennessee and went to Lingleville, Erath County, Texas.

Laura Lou Kirk was born in Lewis County, Tennessee, in 1880, in the south central part of the state. Her parents, Robert Kirk and Mary Ellen Pollock Kirk, moved with their children to Lingleville, Texas.

Laura Kirk, their second child and oldest daughter, was only twelve years old when her father died. In 1898, Laura, age eighteen, married Perry Lovick Peeples, who was twenty-three. They remained in Lingleville near her mother for a few years and then they bought a farm in Eastland County, seven miles from the town of Eastland. When they moved to Eastland County, Cecil Edward Peeples, the second of their six sons,

3. Perry Lovick Peeples and Laura Kirk were married in 1898.

was about two years old. So he spent most of his childhood on that farm. He attended school in a one-teacher school a few miles from his home and remembered his teachers there as encouraging him in his love of reading.

While the family lived in Eastland County, every member worked in the field. However, the mother was also the one who kept the house, cooking the meals, cleaning, washing, ironing, and making some of the clothes. Because there

3

were no girls in the family, Cecil as the second son evidently was the one chosen to help his mother when she had to have some help. He would wash or dry dishes after the noon meal and then go to the field when she did. That arrangement seemed to give him additional understanding of her work. He was always very thoughtful about how much work there was in house-keeping.

After the family moved to Lubbock County, farm work was very different for them. The fields were irrigated and most of the work was done with machinery. Laura did not work in the fields there.

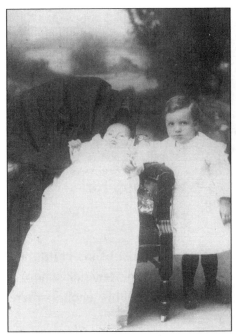

Courtesy of Gladys Peeples

4. Infant Cecil Edward Peeples with his two-year old brother, Lois Peeples, in 1902.

Because the youngest of the three older boys in the family was eight years old when the next son was born, they were almost like two families. In some ways, the younger ones were more like nephews to the older brothers. They spent little time at home together, the older ones being away in school or at work much of the time. However, there was always a feeling of close kinship, and through the years, reunions

4

were regular and frequent.

***

As a fourteen-year-old boy, Cecil Peeples walked seven miles to school, day after day, tired, no doubt, in the evening from a ball game or practice. No wonder that at times he had stopped at a house where an old man, who often could not sleep, had sat on the porch smoking his pipe, happy to tell an interested boy about his experiences in the Civil War. He made the reading of history more meaningful.

Courtesy of Gladys Peeples

5. Cecil Peeples, age two, and Lois Peeples, age four, in 1904.

Other people in that community had contributed to this boy's love of learning. Teachers encouraged him. Visiting ministers, entertained in the Peeples home, enjoyed passing on books they read to a boy so eager to read. By the time he was fourteen years old, Cecil had decided he wanted to become a preacher.

By 1918 the Ranger Oil Field had been developed so much that there was even a gushing well brought in on the Peeples peanut farm. Everyone seemed to be engaged in oil field work. Cecil worked as long as thirty-six hours at a time without sleep. Life had changed. When the family thought about school for that year, they faced a serious problem. The Eastland school, adequate for a few hundred students, must now enroll thousands. There was no way it could meet the challenge. That was the reason the Peeples family decided to send Cecil to Meridian College where there was an academy teaching high school students on the same campus with the junior college students. He enrolled as a junior in the academy, and before long was also actively involved with the college choral club. Cecil soon became a member of the college debate team. A whole new world was opening for him.

When he returned home at the end of his second year at Meridian, ready to begin college work, he found that home was not Eastland, but Idalou. His family had sold their Eastland property and bought land in Lubbock County, nine miles from the little town of Idalou near the city of Lubbock. In the Methodist Church at Idalou, Clarendon College, not Meridian, was the school the ministers talked about. Clarendon College belonged to the Northwest Texas Conference of the church; Meridian belonged to the Central Texas Conference. I suppose that it was almost inevitable that Cecil would enroll in Clarendon College in the fall of 1920. There he played football as he had at Eastland, but a football game injury caused him to lose that year. He spent most of the 1920-'21 school year recuperating at home. However, in the fall of 1921 he again enrolled in Clarendon College and had a successful year. Cecil played football, but more importantly, he became a debater for his literary society and for the college. He took part in dramatic club productions and became a member of the college quartet. Those boys sang in churches all over the Texas Panhandle and in eastern New Mexico. They publicized the school and solicited students.

6. Members of the Clarendon College Quartet during the 1922-'23 school year were (l to r) Roy Beights, Bill Craig, Cecil Peeples, and P.W. Walker.

In the summer, the quartet was employed to continue the programs they had been giving, now full time instead of just on weekends. On one of those occasions, they gave their program in the Methodist Church at Texline, Texas, and there Cecil and I, Gladys Labenski, met for the first time.

I had my room reserved at Clarendon College for the fall semester, and my name had been given to the boys of the quartet with instructions to meet me and answer any questions I might have about the school. I actually knew more about them than they did about me, because I had a girl friend a year older than I who was attending Clarendon College,

7

and from her I knew a bit about each member of the quartet.

When school started in the fall of 1922, a busy year began for both Cecil and me. He again played football, this year on a team that went undefeated. He continued to sing with the quartet on weekends. He debated for the college and for his literary society; he received the ring given to the best debater in his inter-literary society debate. He acted in plays given by the drama department and wrote for the press club, all the while carrying a full academic load.

Courtesy of Gladys Peeples

7. Gladys Labenski attended Clarendon College and lived in Texline in the fall of 1922.

I also carried a full academic load including English, Latin, Spanish, history, mathematics, education, and private lessons in speech. I wrote occasionally for the school paper and participated with the literary society in its inter-literary society debate. I received the ring as the best debater on either team.

Busy as Cecil and I were, our paths did cross occasionally. We had walked from the church to the dorm once or twice on Sunday evening. Once after hearing me speak at the meeting of the Epworth League, Cecil had told his roommate that I was the girl he was going to marry some day.

8

When the football season ended and time came for the banquet to celebrate the successful year for the team, the coach called the players together and told them of plans for the banquet. He said that they were inviting as guests at the banquet the girls of the club which was best known for its school spirit in supporting the team. Some of the team had been dating girls in that club, but there were several girls in the club who had been dating boys not on the team. He had put the names of those girls on the board and wanted other team members to volunteer to invite them. Cecil immediately said, "I'll take Gladys Labenski."

Coach Burton said, "Good Sport, Peeps!" and marked off my name.

So it happened that on December 7, 1922, we had our first formal date. For seventy years, we celebrated that as our special day. Not even Pearl Harbor could alter it.

In the fall of 1923, Cecil began his teaching career at Tahoka High School where he coached football and basketball and taught history. The following summer he enrolled at Southern Methodist University. That fall he

Courtesy of Gladys Peeples

8. Gladys taught high school in Texline in 1927.

9

9. Eugene Slater, A.Q. Sartain, Cecil Peeples, and J.J. Morgan were friends during their years at S.M.U. In the background is the "White Elephant," a rooming and boarding house. The child is unidentified.

played football for S.M.U., but by the end of the year he had decided to give up his football scholarship and find other means of financing his education. Perhaps he had simply outgrown the game, become disillusioned about it in the educational process. For the rest of his university career, he used various means of financing his eduction. At times, he worked on the campus in the shrubbery and flower beds. Much of the time he waited tables in a tearoom near the university. For a time he worked as a fireman for the University Park Fire Department. He majored in government for his masters degree and taught a course in government at the university, and he coached debate teams. Of course, he borrowed some money. All the time he was actively involved in choirs and playing roles in the Arden Club productions of plays ranging from those of Shakespeare to those of George Bernard Shaw. However, most of his time he devoted to the courses he took leading to three degrees, bachelor of arts, master of arts, and bachelor of divinity.

During those years, I had been equally busy. I taught one

10. In 1929, Cecil Peeples (left) and Eugene Slater worked and lived at the University Park Fire Station while they attended Southern Methodist University's School of Theology.

year in San Antonio as a regular substitute in a first grade class of Mexican children, and then I spent a year teaching a second grade class in the Texline school. In 1925, I enrolled at S.M.U. as a sophomore, and for two years and two summers, I worked toward my bachelor of arts and master of arts degrees. In 1927, I returned to Texline to teach English in the high school. That year, following the state guidelines, I enabled the fourth year of English in Texline High School to be accredited by the State of Texas.

I returned to S.M.U. for the summer session, and in the fall, went back to Texline to teach another year. The next year, I returned to S.M.U. to complete my work for a permanent teaching certificate and for two degrees, except for the actual writing of my thesis for the master of arts degree in comparative literature. That I would complete by August, 1932.

Cecil and I finished final exams on Friday, August 23, and were married on Sunday morning, August 25, 1929, in the chapel of the School of Theology of S.M.U., Dr. Robert W. Goodloe, officiating.

We then went to Texline, where in September we began our teaching career together. I continued to teach English. Cecil taught history, coached football and basketball, and served as principal of the school. The next year, he was elected superintendent of the Texline Independent District and we remained there another year. We enjoyed those two years, and felt we were gaining skills we would use for a lifetime. However, by the spring of 1931, we felt we were ready to move on to the work we had been training for since 1923 when we first began planning our life together.

We declined the offer to return to Texline at a salary that was tempting, and began making plans for the future. We had written to a great many people who might be able to direct us to an opportunity to serve the church. Late in May, we received a telegram from Guy Wilson, presiding elder of the Nacogdoches District of the Texas Conference of the Methodist Church, offering us a four-point circuit. We had never heard of Guy Wilson, and knew nothing of the churches in that part of the state, but we had said we would go anywhere in the United States where there was a place for us. So we wired Guy Wilson our acceptance, and told him we would be there June 3. He replied by telegraph (most people did not use telephones in those days except for local calls) telling us to come to his parsonage in Nacogdoches to receive directions.

When we drove our little A-Model Ford out of Texline that morning in late May, 1931, we felt much as a parachute jumper must feel when he first steps out of the plane, trusting a parachute to open and carry him safely until his feet are on solid ground.

We had looked forward to this day almost from the time in 1923 when we had begun planning our life together. We would have the degrees we needed in school; we would have paid our debts; we would be able to live on whatever we earned. Our car was paid for, and we had enough money in the bank to support us for a few months. Our life in the pastoral ministry was beginning.

Looking back from the late '90s, I can see that the years between 1931 and 1935 helped prepare us for Lon Morris College, perhaps almost as much as did our teaching years, or even some parts of our college and university years. We were learning more about working together in various situations. For example, shortly after we moved to Garrison, we had gone on Sunday afternoon to Arlam, the country community where Peeples preached in the afternoons of the days he preached at Garrison. There, after church, we were visiting with members of the congregation when a rather elderly little woman I had met a few weeks before approached me somewhat timidly and said, "Mrs. Peeples, I wonder if you and your husband would come by my house some time. I have some money to give to missions."

"Why yes," I replied. "We'll be happy to come. Will tomorrow be a good time?"

She looked a bit surprised, but said yes, that it would be a good time for her. She hesitated and then said, "I have asked other preachers to come, but they never did. I realized then that she thought that a preacher's wife was more likely to take her seriously.

On the way home I told Peeples about her invitation, and he said of course we would go the next day. As we approached her little cottage the next afternoon, I asked, "How much do you think she will give you for the Conference Claims?" Of course, I was sure she did not know to call it Conference Claims. She had said missions.

"I think she will give two dollars and a half," Peeples replied.

"You are not optimistic enough. I think she will give five dollars."

A gentle breeze was blowing and a long line of laundry was waving in the yard by her little house. She had already done a lot of work that day. She invited us in and seated us on straight chairs in the sparsely furnished but neat and clean living room. The house was not painted inside or out, and there was no wall paper. I was not surprised, because I had felt sure she did not have much money. We talked about one thing and another. I asked her whether she would like for me to come for her to attend the women's meeting at the church later in the week. She said that if I would come for her, she could walk home; it was just that she did not feel like walking both ways. It was probably three miles. Of course I told her I would be happy to take her there and home. As we talked, I kept wondering when she would mention the money. We got up to leave, and she followed us onto the porch. We had gone down the steps before Peeples said, "Mrs. Peeples said you wanted to contribute to the Conference Claims. How much would you like to give?"

"I didn't say Conference Claims," she explained. "I said missions. I have only a thousand dollars to give now, and if you will have Brother Wilson come out here with you, I will give you the check."

Peeples thanked her and told her he would call Brother Wilson and ask him to come. Of course we went straight to our telephone and called the presiding elder and asked him to come the next day. He came, and she gave them the check. Bishop Kern told us later that, with that thousand dollars, he was able to keep a mission station in China open, although it had been on the verge of closing. Of course, a thousand dollars in 1931 was much more significant than the same amount would be today. When I have seen some fine Chinese students in Lon Morris, I have sometimes thought their teachers might have been trained in that mission. It is a pleasant thought.

In that same circuit in another church, Mount Enterprise, we met two couples, all public school teachers, who were alumni of Lon Morris College. They became our good friends and we learned from them what Lon Morris College had meant in their lives. It had been to them what Clarendon College and Meridian College had been to us.

In all the churches we served, we worked with groups of young people. We assisted the group in Mount Enterprise in repainting and refurbishing the inside of the church building. We directed skits, produced pageants, built sets, made costumes, directed and acted in plays. We took a group to district camp. In Livingston, Peeples often drove our car to help transport members of the football or basketball team to games in other towns, or took students home when they lived far out of town. Thus, he became a friend of the students. It was all part of his work as a minister.

I have always noticed that one of his strengths was his rapport with all age groups. Having been a coach, he easily identified with Coach Summers in Livingston. Together they often met with players, discussed strategy, and offered suggestions, especially to the quarterback, Howard Martin, who later came to Lon Morris as a student. After he graduated from the University of Texas, he came back to Lon Morris as business manager.

In the home of Coach Summers, the couple's eighteen-month-old son got his share of attention, too. One Sunday, instead of leaving the little boy in the nursery, they took him into the sanctuary, sitting near the back of the room. When Peeples walked into the pulpit to begin the service, everyone heard a delighted little voice exclaiming, "Peekles, Peekles!" Then Coach took his son to the nursery.

During the week before Easter when we were living in Wiergate, Peeples preached a series of sermons for a congregation in another town in the district, and was away from

11. Cecil Peeples (right) rides with one of the Wiergate sawmill administrators to a site where timber is being cut.

home all week. I remained in Wiergate to finish preparations for the services on Easter Sunday. We were presenting the same pageant we had directed in the Garrison church the year before. Rehearsals had been concluded, and all that I had to do that week was to see that the set for the production was finished, that costumes were ready, and that the church was decorated for the special Sunday. Also, I was in charge of the morning service. In the years since, I have substituted for Peeples in many situations, but that was the only time I substituted for him in the pulpit. I suppose that the reason I did it then was simply that he took for granted that I could. So I did. That was the way we always worked together.

We enjoyed the years in the churches we served, but in

1935 a new challenge was offered to us. The Board of Trustees of Lon Morris College began their search for a new president. The school was deeply in debt, and the trustees were debating whether to close it or try to find a way to save it. They decided to try one more time to save it.

The trustees wanted a president who had a master's degree as well as a theology degree. It had always been customary to have a minister as president of the school. Dr. Alexander, who founded the school, had been a minister. But evidently the trustees had decided that the president should also be a teacher. They wanted someone with experience in the administration of more than just a Sunday School. And he should be able to secure financial support. They looked over the list of preachers in the Texas Conference and offered the opportunity to Peeples. Of course, they did not know whether he could raise money, and for that matter, neither did he, but he accepted the challenge.

We recalled Clarendon College and Meridian College. Both had been given up by the church because of financial failures. Neither the Northwest Texas Conference, nor the Central Texas Conference could support a junior college. In the Texas Conference, there was a difference. Oil had been discovered under the red clay, and that had made the conference that owned Lon Morris College possibly the most affluent conference in the Methodist Church. That made accepting the challenge possible.

We knew what a school like this had done for us, and that hundreds like us needed a school that was the bridge between high school and the university. It gave young people the chance to develop their leadership ability while they were freshmen and sophomores instead of marking time for that part of their growth until they were juniors or seniors. We believed it made them much more likely to take places of leadership in the communities they would serve.

Again we were stepping out of that dependable plane, trusting that the parachute would bear us safely to solid ground. But this time we had a baby daughter in our arms. Perhaps our faith in that parachute had grown stronger. So in June 1935 we moved to Jacksonville, and our life on the Lon Morris College campus began.

Shortly after Peeples came to Lon Morris, he spent an entire night in his office in the twin towers building in prayer and meditation about the task he had assumed. When the morning broke he saw the sunrise, and ever after seemed secure in the direction ahead.

As the first two or three years at Lon Morris College passed, Peeples became aware that a major function of his role in the school was counselling. Students needed and sought help to solve their problems. He read everything he could find about it, but felt he needed more. We discussed the situation and decided what we could do about it. In the summer of 1939, with our two little girls, we drove to New York City where Peeples enrolled in Union Theological Seminary on the campus of Columbia University. He took courses in counselling taught by Harrison Elliott, and preaching taught by George Buttrick, and heard sermons by Harry Emerson Fosdick, all of whose books he had read in years past.

Through the years, he continued to read. He took *The Christian Century* magazine and bought and read the best new books in his field. When he visited with other ministers, he always asked what they were reading and he enjoyed looking over their libraries, telling them of books he had discovered. He learned from everyone he met. He did not keep a record of which sermon he had preached at each church he visited, because, he said when he preached there again he would have to prepare a new sermon. He was careful never to quit studying.

Because I know much about the life of Cecil Peeples before he became president of Lon Morris College, I am attempting to record the events which, it seems to me, led him to accept the challenge the Board offered him in 1935.

While I was working on writing these memories, I came across something Zula Pearson wrote, which indicates that perhaps others have thought about how it happened that Cecil Peeples came to Lon Morris College. She wrote:

> I don't know how to say it,
>   but somehow it seems to me
> That Dr. Peeples was stationed
>   where God wanted him to be;
> That the place he filled so ably
>   was the reason for his birth;
> To be President of Lon Morris
>   God sent him down to earth.

Of course I know he could have done other things in other places equally as well. He was asked at one time during his years at Lon Morris to run for Congress. Of course, he did not take that seriously, but he had majored in government and taught a history course at S.M.U. Also, Peeples liked to write. Once while he was at Wiergate, we discussed whether or not he might like to go into religious journalism. He enjoyed writing book reviews for the church press. However, he never seemed to regret his choice to remain with Lon Morris College. He could always see how Lon Morris could serve generation after generation of young people who needed it if enough endowment could be procured to guarantee the future of the college. That was the direction he worked toward during the last years of his life.

Chapter Two

Personalities That Shaped Lon Morris College
by
Jim Crawford

Two truths are illustrated by the history of Lon Morris College: 1) the institution shapes the person; and 2) the person shapes the institution.

In the mid-nineteenth century, public education in Texas was scarce. While the constitutions of both the Republic of Texas and, later, the State of Texas required the state to provide for public education, even through the Civil War, little was done to promote public education.

Education was provided by churches and other charitable organizations. The Masonic Lodges of Texas were by far the largest provider of secondary education in Texas at that time.

In 1854 the Masonic Lodge of New Danville (four miles from Kilgore) organized New Danville Masonic Female Academy. Students paid four dollars a month for tuition, and a fee to board. The principal of the school boarded the girls in his home, and found lodging for the boys in other homes in town.

When a school obtained a noted educator, people would actually move to the town where that person taught so their children would benefit from that teacher's skill.

The Rev. Isaac Alexander (1832-1919) was one of the first principals of New Danville Masonic Female Academy. He quickly gained fame across East Texas as one of the outstanding educators in the area.

23

New Danville continued as a female academy until 1873. When the International and Great Northern Railway chose to bypass New Danville and go through Kilgore, the people of New Danville soon began to move nearer the railroad. Jay Gould sold parcels of land near the depot; and as Kilgore grew, New Danville declined.

Methodists in Kilgore wanted to have a school, and formed the Kilgore Society of the Methodist Episcopal Church, South, for the purpose of bringing a school to the township.

Rev. Alexander, who had left New Danville years earlier, was persuaded to be the principal of the newly established school, and it was named Alexander Institute at that time. It was operated privately for two years, but ownership was passed to the East Texas Conference of the Methodist Episcopal Church, South, in 1875.

Another change that took place at about the same time was the admission of males to the Institute. The original school building was one large room with a stage for the teacher's desk and chair. The remainder of the room was divided by a wall that extended to the ceiling separating girls from boys, though both could see the teacher's desk.

Courtesy of Lon Morris College

12. Dr. Isaac Alexander

The Alexander Institute continued through the '80s and into the '90s.

In 1887, Isaac Alexander became the president of the Institute, and held that title through 1890. Because of poor health and

24

tragedies in his family, he retired in 1890, but continued to serve on the Board of Trustees through the remainder of his life.

In 1894, the East Texas Conference of the Methodist Episcopal Church, South, elected to move Alexander Institute to a more central location in the Conference. Bids from Palestine, Rusk, Jacksonville, and Marshall were considered. Jacksonville had no school at that time, and there was an effort by the citizens of Jacksonville to bring back education to their city. When the City of Jacksonville offered to raise the money to construct buildings for the new campus, the Conference decided to relocate Alexander Institute to Jacksonville.

The people of Kilgore, not wanting to give up their school, determined to keep Alexander Institute, and asked the Conference to return it to the Kilgore Society. Because of the confusion of having an Alexander Institute in both Kilgore and Jacksonville, the East Texas Conference voted in 1905 to change the name to the Miller Collegiate Institute. An amendment to the motion suggested the name become the Alexander Collegiate Institute, and the motion passed.

As the school grew and added more of the academic requirements for college credit, Alexander Collegiate Institute applied for and received accreditation as a Junior College.

In 1913, the name was changed once again. Progress had been made to extend the curriculum to include courses at the Junior College level. So the name became Alexander College. That name was used until 1924 when a benefactor, R.A. (Lon) Morris (1846 -1931), a banker from Pittsburg, Texas, offered to pay off the schools indebtedness and build a girls dormitory. Morris' offer was accepted, and Lula Morris Hall was built in memory of his wife. Soon, Morris suggested that he would contribute his entire estate to Lon Morris. There

13. R.A. (Lon) Morris

were two stipulations: first, the school would be renamed Lon Morris College, and second, the school would provide for his welfare for the remainder of his life. Because this estate was valued at more than $200,000, the school chose to follow Morris' wishes, and the name came to be Lon Morris College.

In 1935, Cecil Edward Peeples was elected President of the College. It was a most propitious decision on the part of the Texas Annual Conference and the Lon Morris Board of Trustees.

It has been said "Losers quit when they get tired; victors quit when they win." Victors are victors, not because of their trophies, but because of their character and courage and determination.

Dr. Peeples could not have come to Lon Morris at a worse time. The school was heavily mortgaged. America was in the throes of the Great Depression. Threat of a world war was already being noised across Europe. A person of any less stature than Dr. Peeples would have chosen to abandon the school and its great history.

But my premise from the beginning is that institutions shape the person, and persons shape the institution. To understand the character and courage of Dr. Peeples is the work of other chapters in this book. To understand the institutional character and courage of Lon Morris College that challenged Peeples to stay until he won . . . that is the task of this chapter.

Several personages need to be highlighted. There are too many to cover in the few pages allowed here, but no understanding of the school would be complete without some detail of Isaac Alexander, W.K. Strother, R.A. (Lon) Morris, Jennie Tapp, and T.E. Acker.

Isaac Alexander was born July 24, 1832, in Virginia. He arrived in Henderson, Texas, in 1854. He was 22 years old, had completed a master's degree at Emory and Henry College in Abingdon, Virginia. His brother was the pastor of the Methodist Church in Henderson, and Isaac was licensed to preach in Henderson the year he arrived.

Alexander came to Texas to be a teacher in the Fowler Academy in Henderson, and he began a career of education and ministry in East Texas that spanned 68 years. He was married in 1857 to Sallie Hall. They had three children, two of whom grew to adulthood. Sallie Hall Alexander died in 1864.

Alexander married Margaret Likens in 1870. They had two children, one of whom grew to adulthood.

Isaac Alexander served numerous appointments in the Methodist Church, including the Methodist/Presbyterian Church in Kilgore. He also served in Tyler, Palestine, and Longview, to mention a few.

Alexander was noted as one of the best educators in Texas. He believed in firm discipline, study by recitation, and a strong devotional life. Students were required to attend chapel every day. The typical school day lasted from eight o'clock in the morning until five or six o'clock in the evening.

In Kilgore, Alexander built a large home in which the female students were lodged. The male students were boarded in private homes in the town. At night, the Rev. Mr. Alexander would walk through the streets of town, making sure his boys were behaving themselves as gentlemen.

R.A. (Lon) Morris was a banker and local preacher in Pittsburg, Texas. He was a beneficent man who supported Southwestern University, Southern Methodist University, and the Board of Missions.

Because of his friendship with Isaac Alexander, Morris came to know the dire circumstances of Alexander Collegiate Institute and wanted to help the school. As mentioned earlier, he paid off the indebtedness of the school and built a dormitory, Lula Morris Hall, in honor of his wife. After her death, he agreed to bequeath his entire estate to the school if the trustees would rename the school Lon Morris College, and if the school would provide for his care as long as his lived. Thus, the name of the college became Lon Morris College as it is today.

Another person who assisted in the endowment of the school was Miss Jennie Tapp of New Boston, Texas. In a handwritten will, she left her estate to her church in New Boston (the congregation subsequently built a new structure and named it Tapp Memorial Methodist Church); the Methodist Church in Maud, Texas; and to "Georgetown College" and "Jacksonville College." This created a problem. The two schools were to receive $100,000 each. There was only one college in Georgetown, Southwestern University (a Methodist institution), so the will presented no problem there. However, in Jacksonville there was a Jacksonville College owned by another denomination as well as Lon Morris College (a Methodist institution). When the other college threatened to sue for the estate, Lon Morris College agreed to halve the endowment with that school.

The gifts of Mr. Morris and Miss Tapp were two of the

first that led to the establishment of endowments that have served students through more than a half century.

Among the many presidents who have served Lon Morris College, only one served the school on two separate occasions. W.K. Strother was president of Chappell Hill Female College in 1904 when he was brought to Alexander Collegiate Institute to be its president. He served for five years during this term. At this time the college was expanded to meet the rising demands of a growing student body. Two temporary buildings were constructed for music and the arts.

In 1906 the concrete blocks for the Main Building were being made. Over the next two years, President Strother supervised the construction of the building that was fondly called "The Twin Towers," and that cost $50,000 to build. It stood as the focal point of the campus until 1960 when it was razed and the present administration building was constructed.

President Strother resigned in 1909 to assume the presidency of Western College in Artesia, New Mexico. In 1915, he returned to Alexander and served again as president for three years. In 1916, the college was in debt. President Strother appealed to the East Texas Conference, and the conference voted to issue $20,000 in bonds to retire the debt.

The final personality to be mentioned in this chapter is T.E. Acker. Tom Acker came to Jacksonville in 1907 to attend Alexander Collegiate Institute. He completed his studies at ACI and then attended Southwestern University where he graduated.

Acker was elected mayor of Jacksonville in 1919, and served in that capacity for 34 years. In 1921, he was one of the organizers of the Guaranty State Bank, which had a number of name changes over the years. In 1933, he was elected

14. T.E. (Tom) Acker

president of the bank and served in that capacity until 1948, when he was elected Chairman of the Board. In 1952, he was elected Senior Chairman and served there the remainder of his life.

Tom Acker was elected to the Board of Trustees at Alexander College in 1919 and served for several years as its secretary. He was elected chairman of the Lon Morris Board of Trustees in 1937, and held that title until 1972.

One other fascinating thing to observe about T.E. Acker is that he served as a member of the General Conference of the Methodist Episcopal Church, South, the Methodist Church, and the United Methodist Church, beginning in 1922 and including every General Conference through the 1968 Uniting Conference that brought into being the United Methodist Church. He also was elected to the 1970 special session of the General Conference.

This is hardly more than a thumbnail sketch of several personalities who shaped the institution led by Cecil E. Peeples for 38 years. Yet each of them possessed the character and principles that endowed Lon Morris College with something money cannot buy, the will to survive, the will to achieve, and the will to shape lives with that same character and value.

It was into that climate that Cecil E. Peeples came in 1935, to build on that foundation and to leave on it his own indelible and indefatigable spirit.

The Presidents of Lon Morris College

Isaac Alexander	1873-1890
G.J. Nunn	1890-1896
E.R. Williams	1896-1904
W.K. Strother	1904-1909, 1915-1918
F.E. Butler	1909-1911
J.M. Barcus	1911-1912
M.L. Lefler	1912-1914
J.B. Turrentine	1914-1915
R.G. Boger	1918-1923
G.F. Winfield	1923-1928
E.M. Stanton	1928-1932
H.T. Morgan	1932-1935
C.E. Peeples	1935-1973
J.E. Fellers	1973-1976
Faulk Landrum	1976-1992
Chappell Temple	1992-1994
Clifford Lee	1994-Present

Chapter Three

A Young President And A Bankrupt College
by
Wayne C. Odom

Growing up in the small town of Jacksonville with many relatives and family friends related to Lon Morris College, I cannot remember when I first became aware of Cecil Peeples. Perhaps it was seeing him at First Methodist Church, or recognizing him as a friend of my parents, or discovering that he was the college president when, as a very young boy, I began taking special lessons from Zula Pearson and appearing in dramatic productions at the college. In preparing these pages, it was a great surprise to discover how young he was when he became president of Lon Morris. I grew up without ever questioning the very natural expectation that upon completing high school, I would begin college in my home town.

With the invitation to be one of the participants in producing this book, I went back to the college archives and read the minutes of meetings of the Board of Trustees, and interviewed Gladys Peeples and others. I wanted to set the memories and impressions of my childhood and youth, along with the growing affection of more mature years, in some kind of logical order as a tribute to a remarkable life.

What many of us will remember as we think of Cecil Peeples is a life of great purpose. He had a cause: Lon Morris College. He was not Lon Morris, yet for many he was its living embodiment. Since the Lon Morris cause was so central for him, he appeared to be living in a seemingly one-track dimension. If a student's course, whether enrolled in the college or engaged in living long years after college life was over, took a direction he questioned, that student might be asked to give an accounting to Cecil Peeples.

Along with many strongly held values, there was compassion for his fellow human beings. There was patience. There was the fervent wish that life at its best would not pass by any of God's creatures. At the heart of his approach to life, there was steady, continuing kindness. There was a deep caring for people that even enemies could not doubt was genuine.

So many of the struggles of his early years can now be recognized as preparation for giving leadership to a bankrupt church college in the middle of the Great Depression. In order not to begin his pastoral ministry with the burden of indebtedness, he and Gladys taught school in the Texas panhandle following the completion of their studies at Southern Methodist University. But his calling was the ministry of the Methodist Church, and so he made contact with leaders in the Texas Conference, that area of Texas that includes Houston and East Texas. A telegram came from the presiding elder of the Nacogdoches District, Rev. Guy Wilson, inviting him to become the pastor of the Garrison Circuit that included four churches: Garrison, Arlam, Concord, and Mt. Enterprise.

Cecil and Gladys had never been east of Dallas, but they responded in faith, and drove to Nacogdoches. After receiving instructions from Presiding Elder Guy Wilson, they made their first trip to their new parsonage home.

On the Garrison Circuit, the Peeples met two couples who were graduates of Lon Morris. From them, Cecil and Gladys received their first knowledge of that part of God's Kingdom that would consume their lives. Gladys Peeples remembered, "They felt about Lon Morris the way we felt about Clarendon College."

Eighteen months on the Garrison Circuit, one year at Weirgate, eighteen months at First Methodist, Livingston – four years of pastoral experience were part of the life of Cecil Peeples. In the spring of 1935, Peeples was given the greatest challenge of his professional life – the invitation to become president of Lon Morris College.

Alexander Collegiate Institute, as it was called when it was first begun in Kilgore in 1873, was the creation of Dr. Isaac Alexander, an outstanding early Texas Methodist educator and minister. It was moved to Jacksonville in 1894. Its charter stated that it was "the property of the East Texas Conference of the Methodist Episcopal Church, South."

In 1924, facing pressing financial needs (not unusual in the school's history!), Rev. Lon Morris was presented to the Board of Trustees. The school owed $25,000 besides the bonded indebtedness. Rev. Lon Morris, who had been a banker and landowner in East Texas, proposed that if the Board would raise the $25,000, he would give the school "$50,000 or $100,000", provided the Board would change the school's name to Lon Morris College.

A flurry of activity must have occurred after this announcement. Rev. Glenn Flinn led the effort to raise $25,000 through Texas Conference churches. President G.F. Winfield, only one month later, could report to the Board that the $25,000 had been raised (or at least promised). On July 10, 1924, T.E. Acker, secretary of the Board, appeared before a notary public in Cherokee County to make the official name change to

Lon Morris College.

Before Cecil Peeples came to the school, many outstanding presidents preceded him. In the 1920s and 1930s, such men as G.F. Winfield and E.M. Stanton, Jr., guided the college through difficult and challenging times. Buildings were constructed, indebtedness was confronted, and funds were raised. But above all, students were educated, teachers were hired, and college life was built up. Annual bulletins reporting on college life in those years bear a remarkable resemblance to what was happening in the lives of students in more recent years. Courses were offered comparable to those offered in the strongest universities in the State of Texas. College life showed a great variety: speech, drama, sports, social clubs, religious organizations, choirs, orchestras, and various kinds of clubs. President Winfield said of Lon Morris that "its chief values are human values." Lon Morris, through the many years of its existence, went a long way in the direction of realizing this description.

In 1935, at the height of the Depression, the school's finances were in a desperate condition. Closing the school had been discussed but not acted upon.

The Lon Morris Board met at the Palace Cafe in Jacksonville on June 14, 1935. T.E. Acker, reporting for the nominating committee, said there was unanimous support for Cecil Peeples to be the new president of Lon Morris. Peeples was called in, and, according to the Board minutes, "made a brief statement expressing his appreciation to the Board."

He was 32 years old. His possession of a master's degree and his teaching experience, unusual among ministers at that time, must have brought him to the attention of the Board. Whatever he had learned as a minister in the Methodist

Church, as a teacher, as an outstanding student, as an administrator was now to be tested in his new, difficult assignment.

The young president was a visionary in many ways, but he was also practical. He knew there were a number of strong resources on his side. Gladys remembers how he was well aware that Lon Morris was the only Methodist college within the borders of the Texas Conference. The school was owned by the Texas Conference, as its charter stated. And, in spite of the Depression, the area comprising the Texas Conference had oil – lots of it. Whether or not the monetary resources within the bounds of the Conference could be channelled toward Lon Morris remained to be seen, but there was no doubt in Cecil Peeples' mind that the resources were there. For him, there was always more good news than bad. It was his job to live in the confidence that everything he really needed was already there. Problems and difficulties were to be met with the confident understanding that they were, in principle, already overcome.

One of the first financial actions carried out by Peeples was part payment on all the bills Lon Morris owed. (And, according to Gladys, "Lon Morris owed everybody.") With only a few thousand dollars with which to do this, he at least made *some* payment on every bill. He also included a letter in which he acknowledged that this was not full payment. Yet he made it clear he would not be satisfied until every dollar that the college owed could be paid. Rather than receiving disgruntled, unhappy replies, the responses he received were very gratifying. In the tough times of the Depression, it meant something that he was trying. A number of letters were written to Peeples expressing appreciation that he was doing the best he could.

This practice continued. Whatever money was available was apportioned to all the existing bills. Progress reports were given to creditors describing the financial situation of the college. People were told what steps were being taken to meet the college's financial difficulties. Without a doubt, these creditors would have preferred full payment. But the courageous way in which the new president took full responsibility for what was owed to them, plus struggling each month to pay them all he could, must have given them hope that, with much patience on their part, they would eventually be paid.

Cecil and Gladys Peeples did not escape financial troubles themselves in their first year at Lon Morris. During the first summer in 1935 they were to receive $90 a month in salary. As a matter of fact, they actually received $75 a month. However, teachers could eat in the dining hall as part of their salary. So they, along with the other teachers, endured these difficult times in the life of the college.

When they first arrived at the school, the Peeples moved into a college-owned house at 502 Devereaux in Jacksonville. There was very little furniture in the house, since the Peeples had made a decision not to buy the furniture owned by the previous president. Gladys remembers being embarrassed by a visit from Mrs. C.D. Molloy and Mrs. I.T. Shotwell. There was not even enough furniture to invite her guests to sit down. But as time went on, the situation was remedied. Gladys built bookshelves and cabinets. Miss Lottie Williamson, in the business office, helped by finding a table and some chairs. Gladys says they improvised and were rather creative when it was necessary, but they were happy with the challenge.

Nelda Peeples Darrell, looking back on her years as a child at Lon Morris, has many happy memories. She says:

Dedicated as my dad was (and my mother, too) to Lon Morris, he was still very much a family man, and we, his daughters, did not feel neglected. Instead, we felt Lon Morris was the most important institution in our lives, too. I always felt I could never marry someone who hadn't gone to Lon Morris, because he wouldn't realize how special it was. The story has been told many times that when I was two and my little sister was born, I wanted to name her Lon Morris College. When my parents didn't cooperate, I still stubbornly told people her name was Geraldine Lon Morris College.

We were in the children's theater under Mrs. Pearson; we went to almost every production of every play, and to the state one-act play tournaments, and the away-dramas in churches; we attended every choir concert and every recital, taking piano and voice lessons at the college ourselves when we were old enough. We were mascots for sororities. We ate lunch every day, even during our school days, in the Lon Morris cafeteria. It was part of my dad's salary. We felt sorry for the other little girls who didn't belong to Lon Morris College.

Daddy unwound after a tense week by taking us to the double feature at the Palace Theater. We went almost every Saturday afternoon. Practically any night he was in town, he could be talked into driving us around town before we went to bed, seeing the newest buildings being built and often ending up at the train depot to watch the Eagle come by at 7:50.

We had looked forward to going to Lon Morris for so long that I hardly could think what to do with the rest of my life when my years there were finished. Almost all of my dreams had already come true. Both of us did marry Lon Morris exes. Though we lived too far from Lon Morris to send my sister's two boys and my four children to school there, all of them have grown up knowing what a special place it was for us.

Courtesy of Gladys Peeples

15. Nelda gets to go with Daddy, but Gerri can't because she's been sick – and she's about to cry! (1940)

Knowing that Lon Morris "owed everybody," Gladys was hopeful that in the fall, with school starting again, things would be better. It can also be said that the hopeful outlook of Cecil and Gladys Peeples was a very important new resource given to the college in that summer of 1935.

Numerous Board meetings were held that first year. A plan of action to be presented to Annual Conference in the fall was in the hands of Rev. Glenn Flinn, who had been of much help to the college in the past. On December 18, a meeting was held to consider a letter from the Metropolitan Insurance Company in St. Louis, the company owning Lon Morris' bonded indebtedness. No action was taken, possibly because there were few available resources to meet this demand.

Yet, by the time of the annual Board meeting on May 21, 1936, Dr. Peeples was able to report "a very successful year." In the matter of finances, the college was reported to have "held its own." T.E. Acker and Rev. Lewis Nichols, pastor of First Methodist Church in Jacksonville, praised the work of both Dr. Peeples and Wayland Moody, business manager of the college. "A successful year," it was said. "One of the greatest in the history of the college." Perhaps the words that sum it up best are the words of Gladys Peeples who, looking back on that time, said "By the end of the first year, we knew we could do it."

At a special meeting of the Board on September 8, 1936, Dr. Peeples' proposal for an "Out of Debt Committee" was accepted. R.W. Fair, a prominent oil man in Tyler, was the chairman of the committee.

Dr. Peeples proposed raising one hundred scholarships of $90 each. The plan was for the students to use the money from the scholarships while signing a note payable to the college's endowment fund. The note was to be repaid after the student completed his or her years of education.

A plan was also presented to cover all current bills of the college, estimated to be $20,000. The difficult matter of meeting the bonded indebtedness was addressed by asking for a special committee to go to St. Louis to have conversations with the bond company.

An ambitious plan of action was then voted. In the next five years, $250,000 was to be raised: $60,000 for outstanding debts, $90,000 for new buildings, and $100,000 for the endowment fund.

A $75,000 goal, to be raised on a Sunday in the church year called College Day, was also approved. This money was to be used to pay the most pressing debts. In addition, the Jacksonville District, where Lon Morris was located, was given a "Lon Morris challenge." The challenge was to raise $1 for each $4 raised in all the other nine districts of the Texas Conference. A committee was set up in each district to carry out this project.

Not all of these plans were completed as planned. Not all achieved their stated goals. But the vigorous, strong initiative behind these plans was significant. Methodist people in the Conference saw there was a strong effort to breathe new life into Lon Morris. It was becoming a different place. Instead of the gloom of a threatened closing, there was a new, confident spirit.

Finding and keeping good teachers was an important aspect of this new spirit. Cottages were built for teachers. Even if salaries were low, the combination of having a place to live and access to the Lon Morris dining hall brought security to the teachers. As some teachers expressed in later years, their salaries, when you considered the addition of food and lodging, were comparable to other institutions of higher learning at that time.

Dr. Peeples tried a number of ideas to help the college

survive. There was the dairy, for example, in which college boys worked a number of hours each day, giving them income to stay in school and providing the Lon Morris dining hall with dairy products. And the dining hall was enriched by all the vegetables grown on the farm.

There was the $10 Club idea. Approved by the Board on May 23, 1939, it called for one hundred people to give $25 and one thousand people to give $10. Jacksonville Board members proposed advertising the $10 Club in Jacksonville, giving local citizens a part in helping save the college.

By the time of the Board meeting of May 22, 1939, T.E. Acker, who had become chairman of the Board in 1937, could take what might seem a risk with the Board. With Dr. Peeples outside the room, he asked Board members to give their opinion of the work of Cecil Peeples. He must have known what he would receive. There was a unanimous expression of support for Cecil Peeples' successful leadership of the college. Rev. Bradley led in prayer, giving thanks for Dr. Peeples and the college. When Dr. Peeples rejoined the meeting, he was told of the unanimous expression of appreciation by the Board. As always, he responded by thanking the Board for their support and their many ways of helping to sustain the college.

Bringing the Navy pilot training program to Lon Morris in World War II brought an influx of both students and money. Jesse Jones of Houston, a member of Roosevelt's Cabinet, was contacted by Bishop A. Frank Smith about locating the flight school at Lon Morris. Wallace Phillips was the leader of this important program.

On May 25, 1942, Dr. Peeples was elected to a three-year term, the first time this had happened. His salary was never large. At the annual Board meeting in 1945, his salary was raised to $4,250 a year, still less than one president's salary in the early 1920s. In 1947, it was raised to $5,000. By 1950, the salary was set at $6,000. In all the years of his leadership, he never received a salary of more than $16,000. This no doubt reflected his belief, formed from his early decision to follow the example set by George Washington, that a leader's task is to serve. He focused for a number of years on paying off the debt. He evidently felt he could best accomplish this by taking as little as possible for himself.

The Texas Conference, owner of Lon Morris, was the main boundary of Dr. Peeples' efforts to support the college. Although he visited Dallas and other places outside the Conference, he respected the fact that other Methodist institutions were in those areas. Knowing Lon Morris was a Texas Conference institution, he focused on this as his target area.

Various drives to support Lon Morris were voted by the Texas Conference. In 1960, a notable event in Texas was the $32 million dollar goal, set by all the Texas Methodist conferences. The purpose was to raise capital funds for all Methodist schools in the state. Lon Morris' share, – a few hundred thousand dollars, was applied to the debt.

Perhaps the most important gift the Conference made to Lon Morris was granting Cecil Peeples the privilege of contacting individuals and institutions within the bounds of the Conference. No one questioned, for example, the right of the Lon Morris choir to visit a church in Houston, with Dr. Peeples going along to give his much-repeated speech, well known to his ex-students: "Three ways to help Lon Morris."

One of the ways was to give to the endowment fund of the college. Many times, Dr. Peeples expressed what he saw happening with church colleges in every part of the nation.

He saw that only the well-endowed colleges survived. And in the case of a junior college like Lon Morris, the situation was even more urgent. He saw the collapse of church junior colleges everywhere along with the rise of more inexpensive state schools.

With an endowment, he explained, the college could use the interest it earned for operating expenses. If the endowment fund itself was never touched (something Dr. Peeples believed in like a sacred principle), the college could go on operating for years. Increasing the endowment fund, then, was a very important way of saving Lon Morris.

Making a thoroughly accurate assessment of all Cecil Peeples accomplished in his lifetime is a difficult assignment. For some, what he accomplished for the school is rightly seen as a remarkable achievement. For those who viewed him from a distance, his clear, crisp speaking style and boundless enthusiasm will be remembered. For those who knew him well, there was that steady, continuing concern, those strongly-held values, and that irrepressible confidence. He touched the lives of many. He invested himself in serving an institution he deeply loved, and he inspired numbers of people to join in this cause with him.

The Lon Morris choir used to sing what he told us was his favorite song: "There's A Long, Long Trail A-winding." He gave a humorous reading, accompanying the song. In at least some ways, his reading was comparable to a rap song of today. He may or may not have brought this reading to us from his days in Clarendon or S.M.U., but whatever the source, the choir's program, more often than not, would end in this lighthearted way. The smiles on the faces of the audience said as much as anything could say it, that the people listening were having a great time, and that they would remember our singing as something that was a lot of fun. (This happened, of course, only *after* he was sure they'd heard "three ways to help Lon Morris"!)

He had walked a long trail to realize his goal of an excellent school of higher learning, paid for, with an endowment to help secure its future. On the way, he found people he cared for, whom he inspired to become all they could become.

"There's a long, long night of waiting,
Until my dreams all come true,
Till the day when I'll be going down
That long, long trail with you."*

---

* From "The Long, Long Trail" by Stoddard King, written in 1913. Set to music by Alonzo Elliott.

16. The brothers are (front l to r) **Cecil Peeples (2nd born), Clyde Peeples (3rd), Lois Peeples (1st), (back l to r) Vance Peeples (6th), Perry Lovick "Pete" Peeples Jr. (5th), and Glenn Peeples (4th). Picture is from late 1940s.**

47

17.
Cecil and Gladys
Peeples with
teenage
daughters,
Gerri and
Nelda, in
1950.

Chapter Four

Developing And Challenging A Faculty
by
Walter L. Harris

Institutional loyalty and commitment were faculty hall-marks during the thirty-eight years of the Peeples administration. Over the years the faculty and college staff came to reflect the influence of Cecil Peeples in the selection process, but if he found a single area of great strength when he arrived at Lon Morris in 1935, it was definitely the faculty. Several members of the faculty he inherited in 1935 were still on board fifteen years later in the early 1950s. Arch Pearson, Zula Pearson, Nancy Perry, Henry Robinson, Donnella Smith, and Lottie Williamson were core members of a faculty that survived intact through the Great Depression, World War II, and well into the post-war era. Over the years Cecil Peeples was instrumental in recruiting many other faculty members, and in expanding the roles and influence of those he found in place.

Faculty compensation, at least the monetary aspect of it, was scant during the Great Depression and did not improve much until well after World War II. But cash salaries did not tell the whole story, because the overwhelming majority of faculty members lived in housing furnished "at the convenience of the employer" and ate many of their meals, including meals for family members, on the same basis. It was not until the decade of the 1960s that the practice of meals in the college cafeteria began to give way to an adjustment in cash compensation in lieu of college-furnished board. At about the same time, the college began adjustment of cash salaries to move away from the "convenience of the employer" principle.

Especially in the early Peeples years the compensation of faculty had to compete as a priority with insufficient funds for building maintenance and the seemingly unending demands of creditors from all directions. After about 1957 faculty salaries were somewhat more competitive with public education than previously, and they remained so throughout the 1960s and until Peeples' retirement. They probably would not have been competitive, however, without such widespread provision of faculty housing and meals. Well into the 1960s much of the food was supplied by the college farm, with a significant part of the farm work done by students on scholarship.

The core faculty of the Peeples era was an amazing and committed group of professionals. During all the years of Cecil Peeples' association with Lon Morris College the college was blessed with a remarkable richness of academic talent and capabilities. A potpourri of human personalities continuously made possible unique contributions to the college and to the lives of its students.

Henry V. Robinson had come to Lon Morris in the late 1920s after gaining some teaching and administrative experience in Leon County. He was serving as Superintendent of Schools in Jewett at the time of his move to Lon Morris. He was an easy-going, low profile individual who had a winsome smile and was blessed with near-endless patience. Robinson and his wife Maudine were a prominent part of campus life at LMC for about 40-years until the time of his retirement in 1969. Maudine Robinson owned and operated a dress shop, "Our Shop," in downtown Jacksonville. Although they had no children they were sometimes affectionately referred to as "Maudine and PawDean" by students in the fifties and sixties. When Robinson retired, he and Maudine remodeled an older home they owned at the corner of College Avenue and Devereaux Street, and lived there until the time of their deaths.

Lottie Mae Williamson taught in the business department and served as Business Manager for the college from soon after 1935 to the time of her marriage in 1960. She was a dedicated part of the core faculty which Peeples found in 1935, and she was a major player in the Peeples effort to restore solvency and to establish financial credibility. Miss Williamson was never married while on the college staff. She dedicated her life to her work and to the care of her aging mother, who lived with her in college-furnished housing. In late 1959, after her mother's death, Miss Lottie met John Cashman of Wessington Springs, South Dakota. They were married in the spring of 1960 and they lived in South Dakota until the time of his death in the late 1980s or early 1990s. Miss Lottie maintained her contact with LMC mainly through their practice of spending the winters in San Antonio, rather than in South Dakota.

Miss Donnella Smith, a teacher of English and mathematics, had been a part of the college staff since the early 1920s and remained until 1952 when she resigned to join the faculty of Bob Jones University in Greenville, South Carolina. Miss Don served in a variety of capacities outside the classroom, including sponsorship of and advisor to Religious Council, Morning Watch, and the college yearbook, *The Alexandra.* She also was the original sponsor of Rho Chapter of Phi Theta Kappa, the national junior college honorary scholastic society. Miss Don was a deeply religious person and a powerful spiritual influence in the lives of hundreds of Lon Morris students across four decades. She may be best remembered for her uncompromising opposition to dancing on campus, a stand which probably hastened her departure when dancing was ultimately permitted as a part of student social life.

Although the role of Donnella Smith was firmly established in the Lon Morris Faculty long before Cecil Peeples came, she continued as a strong and unique force for most of two decades with President Peeples. As the sponsor of Religious Council, which met weekly, she had an opportunity to become closely involved with students; and she did not hesitate to advise them in regard to romance, religion, or anything else. Each semester, a full week was designated as Religious Emphasis Week. While the Religious Council organized prayer groups and supported the Religious Emphasis Week fully, it was President Peeples who selected the guest preachers. Often these special weeks became literally "Revival Meetings" with much of the excitement and fervor that were associated with revival meetings of that era. Speakers for these Religious Emphasis Weeks were chosen by President Peeples from among the pastors of the Texas Conference. Special memories are associated with the preaching of Walter Rabb Willis, W.W. Conerly, Grady Hallonquist, and Emmett Dubberly, some of whom were Lon Morris Alumni. After a few years, the invited speakers for Religious Emphasis Week were individuals who had been students at Lon Morris after Peeples had become president. This group included

John Wesley Hardt, Asbury Lenox, James Lee Riley, Bill Scales, Wayne Odom, and Don Benton. Peeples often attended the weekly meetings of Religious Council, and was always present for the special Religious Emphasis Week activities.

In 1938, among the freshman class was an orphan boy from Buffalo named Burney Cope, who had been out of high school for four years. During the first week of school he had a confrontation with a naive freshman ministerial student, and by the time of the revival week a month or two later, the ministerial student persuaded Burney to attend the revival services. As a complete surprise Burney Cope was converted in that revival, and an unexpected friendship began to flourish between the green freshman and Burney Cope. In their second year they milked cows at the College Dairy, and one went on from Lon Morris to SMU, while Burney Cope went to Southwestern University and began serving churches in the Southwest Texas Conference. Later Burney Cope went to Perkins School of Theology and spent his life as a Methodist preacher in Oklahoma. While some ministerial students turned to other vocations, there is no record of how many Lon Morris students experienced conversions—many of which led them into the ministry of the Church. The relationship of Cecil Peeples to the faculty and the students was clear and strong, especially with regard to church careers decisions.

August of 1938 marked the beginning of one of the most meaningful, lasting, and beneficial relationships developed by Cecil Peeples in his professional career. It was at that time that Wallace A. "Windmill" Phillips and his wife, Annie Laurie, joined the Lon Morris family. Windmill was an assistant coach to Arch Pearson, and Annie Laurie was a dorm matron in Smith Hall, the girls dormitory. Windmill came on board at a salary of a whopping $1,150 per year, plus room and board, and Annie Laurie's salary was set at $25 per month. Together they became a team that would be crucial in the Peeples effort to restore the college to a sound financial footing. They had been teaching in the Titus County community of Cookville, but their Lon Morris ties went back to their student days at LMC in the late 1920s. Annie Laurie remembers that "Windmill was the first boy I met at Lon Morris, although there wasn't any spark or anything at that time." She had come from the little Leon County community of Nineveh. Annie Laurie and Windmill began a relationship with each other and with Lon Morris College that extended across seven decades. By the end of the 1930s the affordability of the football program was seriously in question. With the exodus of male students in the spring of 1942, following Pearl Harbor, the emphasis changed from athletics to utilization of the faculty and facilities in other ways.

In the case of Windmill Phillips, his wartime niche was as operator of the Civil Aviation Authority training program at Lon Morris College. It is both ironic and of historical significance that this program became the vehicle by which almost forty years of accumulated debt was retired, and which enabled the college to maintain a stable male student presence during the years of World War II. Fortunately for LMC, Windmill Phillips had the organizational, personal, and financial skills to direct the program; and fortunately for the Phillips family, that had grown to include two children, Andy and Sissy, the college provided the institutional setting needed for the program's success. With the end of World War II and the onset of veterans' education programs and an assortment of trade schools, Windmill and Annie Laurie went into a number of business ventures that included trade schools, independent oil operation, semi-pro baseball, and others.

Because he recognized Windmill's talent, commitment to the college, and future potential, Peeples quickly brought Phillips onto the board of trustees once he was no longer an employee. When a group of board dissidents attempted to replace Peeples with a new president in the early 1950s, Windmill Phillips was among those who came to Peeples' defense most vigorously and effectively. The Peeples presidency not only survived the assault, but grew stronger because of it. Afterward, Peeples launched the greatest era of building, enrollment growth, and financial security Lon Morris had ever enjoyed. Peeples was able to develop and maintain an amazing level of lay support from faculty, former faculty, and the board.

From the 1920s until her retirement in the 1950s, the college librarian was Mrs. Nancy Perry, the widow of a Methodist minister. She ran "her library" with a stern and disciplined hand and voice. In addition to her other responsibilities, she ran the college bookstore out of one corner of the library in the Twin Towers Building.

For many years Mrs. Perry and Miss Don shared the same duplex on the campus. Although they were quite different in temperament, they demonstrated a common commitment to the well-being of the college and its students. Mrs. Perry was much less inclined than Miss Don to get involved in the activities of student life, at least during the later years of her professional career.

As librarian, one of Mrs. Perry's treasured roles involved conducting a series of "library lessons" for students in Freshman English classes. She developed, in conjunction with the

English teachers, a wide selection of problem-solving exercises that every student in the English classes was required to complete as a component of the grade for the first semester of Freshman English. The library lessons included specific activities from encyclopedias, exercises that required familiarity with the card catalog, the Dewey Decimal System, fiction, biography, current periodicals, and extensive exposure to *Reader's Guide to Periodical Literature.* In a time long before the advent of computer-assisted learning, Lon Morris was giving its students a firm and solid orientation to the library and the use of its resources.

When Mrs. Perry retired, Mrs. Pearl Molloy became librarian. Mrs. Molloy was the widow of C.D. Molloy, business manager of the college in the 1920s. She, too, had been associated with Lon Morris prior to the Peeples era, and rejoined the faculty in the late 1940s as a teacher of Freshman English and English Literature. Mrs. Molloy was small of stature, and tireless in her capacity to help students who sought her assistance. Although she used student graders to assist in "correcting" the papers of her students, Mrs. Molloy insisted that her graders mark grammatical and composition errors by specific reference to the textbook, Harry Shaw's *Complete Course in Freshman English.* Some of her expressions that were well-used but impressive included "Never use a preposition to end a sentence with. That's something up with which I will not put." She was obsessed with the elimination of dangling participles and split infinitives, which supposedly gave her "chills and fever." In composition she was fond of requiring students to provide "concrete examples" related to the subject at hand. Mrs. Molloy remained active in the library until shortly before her death when she was about eighty.

The versatility and flexibility of Gladys Peeples was literally a legend during the Peeples years. In the early years, she taught Bible for Cecil Peeples when his presidential duties conflicted with his teaching duties. Her teaching as a substitute for him was always without pay. It was, after all, a matter of institutional survival. When there was need for extra sections of courses, she rose to the occasion both in the regular term and in the summer session. She taught Bible, Religious Education, Freshman English, and English Literature; and during World War II, she was an instructor in the Naval Cadet training program headed by Windmill Phillips. Only during the last decade prior to her retirement was she paid a salary that even began to approach the level of most full-time faculty members. She always demonstrated the same level of institutional commitment that was so typical of Cecil Peeples. They were, indeed, partners-in-ministry.

Zula Holcomb Pearson was easily the most widely known of all Lon Morris faculty members during the Peeples years. Her reputation as a teacher of speech and drama was legendary, and it remains so today. Her students included L.Q. Jones, Vernon Weddle, Tommy Tune, Sandy Duncan, Amanda McBroom, Margo Martindale, and dozens of others who were successful in theatre, movies, ministry, teaching, law, and many other endeavors.

Ruth Alexander was one of her students, and ultimately a faculty successor to the great drama and speech tradition built by Zula Pearson. Ruth reflects on their wonderful relationship over the years:

I began taking private "expression" lessons from Mrs. Pearson when I was nine years old, and continued them through my two years at LMC. I made many trips to the top floor of the Twin Towers building. Mrs. Pearson was a remarkable woman–dedicated to her field and to her students, and capable of achieving whatever she wished with both. She became a dominant influence on my life. I always called her "Miss Zula" or "Mrs. Pearson." She was always gracious, firm, and in control. She had her own style of teaching, which was enhanced by her lovely voice and laugh. I would never dare to be late or unprepared for lessons or rehearsals anymore than I would have refused to do anything she requested.

I remember only one time when I said "no" to her because I already had a program to do on the day she wanted me to fill in for her. Until her death, I always confided in her my doubts and fears of being able to do what was required and she'd always say, "Well, of course you can do it!" And so, I proceeded to do it.

I remember a week in Evanston, Illinois with Mrs. Kate Shattuck [a cousin of Zula's Mother] when Arch and Zula completed their master's degrees. I was a freshman in high school then. Some years later when I was teaching in Longview High School, I came home for a visit. As I always did, I went out to see Mrs. Pearson. I kept saying "Mrs. Pearson" until she chuckled and said, "Ruth, we've known each other a long time and you're certainly old enough now to call me Zula." It was a stunning thing to realize that in one moment we had passed from "student/teacher" to "friend." And she remained my dearest friend.

She was intense in the love and understanding of

theatre. She was proud of her students and inspired unlimited devotion from them. She was a vital supporter of LMC.

The thing that made it possible for her to spend life doing what she loved to do was the support and adoration of Arch Pearson. She spent hours in rehearsals, days and sometimes weeks at major theatre universities and centers, or in churches, directing productions and workshops. She and Arch were a perfect match. He was a treasure, a unique man with a great sense of humor who never objected to being in the background, but I doubt that he ever learned to relish Shakespeare.

The Fine Arts program at Lon Morris consisted of a great deal more than speech and drama as a stand-alone department. Choral music and piano filled a high profile place in the curriculum. In the 1930s and early 1940s, Miss Thelma Martensen, whose home was in Kansas City, Missouri did much to popularize the school's choir and to establish a tradition of quality choral music, creating a steady demand for the choir's presence in the churches of the Texas Conference. Later, the choral music program was under the able leadership of Gerry Shaw Weatherby, whose choirs continued the Martensen tradition and demonstrated both exceptional quality and showmanship. Beginning in the mid-1950s, the choir was under the direction of Robert Fordyce, a product of the University of Indiana. Fordyce headed the choral music program at the college during the last half of Peeples' 38-year administration.

Piano instruction was headed by Miss Ruth Reaveley in

the early 1950s. Helen Fordyce joined her husband in the music department as a teacher of organ and private piano lessons. For seven years, from 1957 to 1964, the piano faculty was headed by Roger Keyes, also from the University of Indiana. One year after leaving Lon Morris, Keyes joined the faculty of Baylor University, where he has remained for more than thirty years. Keyes, his wife, Mickey, and Helen Fordyce were extensively involved in providing private piano lessons through the college, an instructional arrangement that Helen Fordyce continued for many years after the Keyes left Lon Morris.

Cecil Peeples faced a continuing challenge to pay Zula Pearson enough to keep her from accepting one of the many offers of employment she received from major colleges and universities. She was a national treasure on the college scene, and in retrospect, it is obvious that only her deep and abiding love for Arch and Lon Morris College, and her loyalty and dedication to Cecil Peeples kept her at the college through her whole professional career. Arch's involvement with athletics in the early years, his various roles as coordinator of the college farm and administrative assistant to Dr. Peeples, the oversight of the family land and property near Rusk, and the responsibility he felt toward Zula and their adopted twins, Mike and Molly, all combined to make him very comfortable in Jacksonville. He may have been disappointed at the news of the end of the LMC football program, but like it or not he understood the need for it, and he was loyal to and supportive of Cecil Peeples.

Ed Kiely, an ex-student and prominent Jacksonville business man, recalls in some detail the transition that occurred over the years in the athletic program at the college.

In the fall of 1940, the opening year of Jacksonville's Tomato Bowl Stadium, the Lon Morris Bearcats played their last football game "and forever," as Dr. Peeples put it. Coach Arch Pearson left after the 1940-'41 school year to try his chemistry teaching skills in the pharmacy business at Rusk.

At about the same time, Dr. Peeples encouraged Windmill Phillips to take a contract to conduct the flight training program for Naval Cadets then occupying Lula Morris Hall.

The Navy program brought in much needed revenue for the college and launched Phllips on a successful business career. As a result of this program, the dining facilities in old London Hall were upgraded, and served the school until the construction of Scurlock Center in 1959. Additionally, the Navy program paid for improving the rundown Kiwanis Gymnasium with a new floor, and replacing the old wood stoves with thermostat-controlled gas heaters and a 500-gallon water heater for the dressing rooms. Visiting teams for several years after World War II praised the old gym because it was one of the few places in East Texas where players could shower with plenty of hot water. The naval program improvements made the old wooden structure at least useable through the Bearcat march to basketball prominence under coaches O.P. Adams, Marshall Brown, and Leon Black, until the Vivian and Bob Smith Gymnasium was completed for the 1964-1965 season.

In the 1943-1944 basketball season there were no male teachers with coaching experience left on the LMC campus except for Windmill Phillips, who was occupied with the navy program. Among the small number of male students who were enrolled, eight wished to have a basketball team, and they enlisted one of their own, Ed Kiely, to hold workouts, make substitutions, and schedule games. Equipment was scarce to non-existent when Kiely asked Miss Lottie Williamson, business manager, for a new basketball. "What would it cost?" she asked. "About $12," was Kiely's reply. "The college just doesn't have $12," Miss Lottie responded. Kiely remembers that he had a good laugh about two years later when, on a trip to Tyler, Coach Adams bought one-dozen basketballs. "You may not have a job when we get home," he told Adams. "We can't learn to put it in the hoop unless everybody shoots," was Adams reply.

The "one basketball" team that year made some history, however. They "borrowed" an old one from Jacksonville High School Coach C.P. Moseley. Some weeks later, after beating Tyler Junior College four times, they matched some games with Camp Fannin, northeast of Tyler, which was training 75,000 troops every three months in D-Day preparation. After one of the games at the camp, the officer-in-charge came to the dressing room with two new balls. "Put these in your equipment bag," he said in a sharp Yankee brogue, "You fellows need them worse than the United States Army."

This little 1943-1944 team would bring respect and credit to and for the college in the years to follow. Asbury Lenox, Hooper Haygood, Cecil Reed, and Bill Betts filled many pulpits in the Texas Conference. Jerry Horner served as trainer in the Tyler YMCA; Emmett McKenzie, after a successful stint coaching high school football, became superintendent of one of the schools in the Golden Triangle of southeast Texas. Kiely put in more than 43 years in the commercial printing business in Jacksonville. Finally, there was Johnny Horton of Gallatin. He led the team in scoring with one of the first one-hand jump shots seen in the area. Even the "Yankees" at Camp

Fannin admired his one handers.

It fell Dr. Peeples' lot to expel Horton for failure to attend classes. Horton went on to star on the Louisiana Hayride in Shreveport and the Grand Ole Opry in Nashville as a recording artist and song writer. His "Sink the Bismarck" topped one million in record sales. When Dr. Peeples was reminded that Horton might have a friendly pocketbook toward Lon Morris were it not for his sudden exit, it is believed that expulsions became few and far between, and that the administrative oganization of the college was structured to put this type of discipline at greater distance from the president's office.

Arch Pearson returned to coach the 1944-1945 Bearcats, but rather than going out on the recruiting trail, he was glad to return to full-time teaching when Dr. Peeples landed O.P. Adams from West Texas. Adams' wife had just died, and an apartment in the Lula Morris girls' dormitory gave him a place for his grade school daughter, Shirley, when he was out officiating at football and basketball games or with the Bearcats.

Puerto Ricans on the team were smaller than their Texas counterparts, and Adams' run and shoot style was an immediate hit with them. Alberto Renta, along with Manuel and Louis Iguina were among the first contingent from the island. These players liked Adams' style so well that they got him named to coach one of the top teams in the Puerto Rican summer leagues.

O.P. Adams' basketball success led Dr. Peeples to agree to offer basketball scholarships, something he never intended to do after the close-down of football. Before the establishment of the Texas Eastern Conference, Adams entered Lon Morris in the re-established Texas Conference, which was divided into four zones with winners to meet for a state championship. The site of the playoff was to be determined by the city making the best monetary guarantee. In meeting at Fort Worth's Blackstone Hotel, it appeared that Amarillo was about to submit the top bid. Adams did not want to go to Amarillo, and after a conference with friends, Adams bit his tongue and made a winning bid of $1,500 per team. Dr. Peeples backed him, and with help on ticket sales they not only oversubscribed the quota due the three visiting teams, but the Bearcats won the state championship. R.C. Buckner, president of the Chamber of Commerce, showed the four teams true Jacksonville hospitality by bringing in a catered meal at center court after the final game. The meal was furnished to players, cheerleaders, officials, and some of their followers.

The Bearcats lost the state championship to Howard County the next year, but it only brought out Adams' competitive nature. The next year Lon Morris and Howard County were back in the finals, this time at a neutral site at North Texas State Teachers College in Denton. Adams had the Bearcats primed, and by half-time it seemed to be no contest. Adams seemed unaware. With under two minutes remaining, and a 40-point lead, he confided to a follower at the end of the bench, "I believe we have them."

Before the National Junior College Athletic Association began a national tournament, Coach Marty Karow at Texas A&M sponsored a 16-team junior college tournament. Texas had agreed to test some proposed rule changes, one of which was the penalty box after four fouls as used in hockey. Potota Rameriz was still in the game for Lon Morris with eight fouls when Bo Ousley's southpaw one-hander beat Tyler in the final seconds for the tournament championship. Ousley had a long career in public education, serving much of the time as

High School Principal in the Frankston ISD.

Frances Beall Harris became the first former student of Lon Morris College to join the faculty in the post-World War II era. John Croft, one of Mrs. Harris' students in the mid-1950s, described her as a teacher with a thirst for knowledge who inspired her students to work hard and accept nothing less than excellence. She was always ready to help her students with their academic problems and questions and to consult with them about student life in general.

Mrs. Harris, the former Frances Beall, was a native of Jacksonville, a lifelong member of its First United Methodist Church, and a graduate of Lon Morris. After earning her bachelor's degree from Southwest Texas State Teachers College in San Marcos, she began her teaching career in Kerens, Texas. In 1935, she married Finis Harris and moved back to Jacksonville. She taught in the Jacksonville public schools until World War II, when she became principal of West Side Elementary School. In 1946, she accepted Dr. Peeples' offer to join the faculty at Lon Morris. Shortly thereafter, she completed her master's degree requirements at Stephen F. Austin State University. She did additional graduate study, including work at the University of Birmingham in England.

During her years at Lon Morris, Mrs. Harris taught courses in American history, psychology, elementary education, and English literature. For many years, she served as sponsor of the Lon Morris Chapter of Phi Theta Kappa (the national junior college honorary scholastic society). She was named a Life Fellow by the national organization in honor of her long service and accomplishments. Mrs. Harris died in Jacksonville in March 1994, leaving behind many admiring students and friends.

Another of the really able and dedicated members of the faculty and administrative team in the period from 1953 to Peeples' retirement in 1973, was Wyman Fisher. Fisher joined the Lon Morris staff in the summer of 1953, and was a key player for more than two decades. He came first as a teacher in the business department and in night school, but gradually assumed administrative duties, including the positions of Dean of Men, Dean of Students, Director of Public Relations, and Director of Student Recruiting.

It was Wyman Fisher, more than any other staff member, who relieved Cecil Peeples of the day-to-day work of student recruitment. Peeples had never been at much distance from the student recruitment process. In Fisher, he found an able and trusted assistant who had the skills, work ethic, and institutional commitment needed to go out, tell the Lon Morris story, and in the process put together a quality student body that enabled the college's program to go forward and flourish during the 1960s and early 1970s. The ability to attract quality students and to provide financial aid packages for them increased greatly, due mostly to three new resources: the National Defense Education Act was passed in 1958; the Lyndon B. Johnson administration expanded student financial aid in the 1960s; and the Texas Tuition Equalization Grant Program came into being.

In the Summer of 1957, two faculty additions proved to be of considerable duration, and helped to round out what would become the Peeples administrative team for most of the last half of his presidency. Walter Harris, a 1952 graduate of the college, joined the faculty in June of 1957. Later in the summer of that year, Virgil Matthews, an ordained Methodist minister, joined the staff as a teacher of religious education and as chaplain.

During his first two years at the college, Harris taught social science courses. including Federal government, state government, American history, economics, and history of western civilization. After the passage of the National Defense Education Act of 1958, and with the increasing impact of the National Defense Student Loan Program on the Lon Morris student population, Peeples asked Harris to assume the position of Director of Student Loans and Endowment. Harris had, at first, doubled in a teacher-dormitory supervisor role, but the dormitory responsibilities were relinquished as his administrative duties were expanded. It may well have been the receipt of substantial money through the O.P. Hairgrove Endowed Trust that prompted Peeples to put increased emphasis on endowment funding, and certainly the increase of more than a quarter of a million dollars in loan and endowment assets caused a major reassessment of administrative and investment priorities. Harris served in the dual role of social science teacher and part time administrator until June of 1960 when he assumed the position of business manager, formerly held by Lottie Williamson. For the remainder of the Peeples presidency, Harris continued to teach one or two courses every semester, but after 1960 his administrative role was greatly increased.

Virgil Matthews arrived on campus in late summer of 1957, and assumed the role of chaplain and teacher of religious education. In Matthews, Peeples found a bright young minister and scholar whom he could trust, and to whom he could relinquish some of the overload which the president had taken on of necessity during the Great Depression, and which was continued during the war years, and the immediate post-war period.

In the 1960s there were some additions of former Lon Morris students to the faculty. Jeannie Mae Phifer joined the English department; Richard E. Burton taught history and government; and Ronald Johnson headed the physics department and taught mathematics. Another faculty addition in the 1960s that resulted in a long-tenured relationship was that of Dutton J. Bailes, who headed the business department for many years.

The willingness of Cecil Peeples to delegate both responsibility and authority to his administrative team was well-documented through the later years of his administration. The physical task of administering a college that served a growing enrollment, a rapidly expanding plant, a host of new programs, and a growing endowment fund was such that trusted lieutenants were essential. The chemistry that developed between Cecil Peeples, Wyman Fisher, Walter Harris, and Virgil Matthews was of a high order. Beginning in the early 1960s, Peeples, Fisher, Harris, and Matthews would make the nearly 700 mile drive to Nashville for a week each summer to attend the National Workshop for Administrators of Methodist Junior Colleges. For about a decade this event was a major planning opportunity, and a time for brainstorming and developing ideas for the next year and the years to come. This conference was sponsored by the Board of Higher Education of The Methodist Church, and was of great value in sharing ideas that worked in other junior colleges, and perhaps in avoiding those which had not worked so well. Lon Morris enjoyed a certain uniqueness in these meetings, being the only remaining Methodist junior college west of the Mississippi River.

If the overall impact of the Peeples faculty were to be

assessed in a sentence or two, the description would have to include heavy emphasis on character and commitment. The faculty believed in the unique mission of Lon Morris College. Most faculty members were convinced that their work with Lon Morris students was significant. They were shaping lives, not just minds. So they committed themselves in the service of the school they loved and the students they respected. It is not an overstatement to say that Lon Morris College would not have survived without the dedication of its faculty, that was fiercely loyal to Cecil Peeples and his attempt to save and advance the college. Though often frustrated by the hardships necessarily imposed by him, it was obvious that commitment was as much to him as to the various academic departments. His enthusiasm was contagious. Others were caught up in his courageous vision and the spirit of his hard work. This, more than anything else, kept the doors of Lon Morris College open during those darkest years with the massive threats and challenges they brought.

Chapter Five

On The Road For And With Students
by
John Wesley Hardt

For the first two decades of his presidency at Lon Morris, Dr. Peeples was the recruitment staff, the personnel department, and the counselor for all kinds of emergencies. During the last half of his four decade administration, other faculty and staff shared some of these duties, but until he retired, President Peeples continued a pastoral approach and gave major amounts of time to personal attention for prospective students, current students, and former students.

In the three appointments in East Texas where he was pastor before being appointed to be president of Lon Morris in 1935, Cecil Peeples was respected and trusted by his parishioners. That respect and trust followed him to Lon Morris, and brought students from each of those three appointments, Garrison, Weirgate, and Livingston, to enroll at Lon Morris. In fact, so many students were recruited from Polk County that they were accused by others of receiving special favors, implying that the "Polk County Kids" enjoyed greater privileges than they had earned.

One of these Polk County students was Howard Martin, who had graduated from Livingston High School in 1935, and had been quarterback for the high school football team. Although Martin was not a Methodist, Peeples had been a friend of the football coach and an enthusiastic booster of the high school team, and Martin followed Peeples to Lon Morris. There he became a campus leader, and there he met a

71

Methodist preacher's daughter named Valerie Condrey, whom he later married. After completing further study at the University of Texas, Martin returned to Lon Morris as business manager. Following the outbreak of World War II, he enlisted in military service. When the war was over, he joined the staff of the Houston Chamber of Commerce and participated in the unprecedented growth of Houston during those years. In that role, he wrote materials that were used by chambers of commerce across the nation. He spent many years in prominent roles in the postwar growth of Houston. Through the years, the friendship between Peeples and Howard and Valerie Martin continued to grow. The Martins returned periodically to the campus and to visit with Gladys and Cecil Peeples, always expressing their gratitude and appreciation for the role Lon Morris had played in their lives.

For years, Peeples drove an average of three thousand miles a month, with many of those miles devoted to recruitment of students. More than half his years were spent driving very ordinary cars, before air conditioning of cars was popular. Long before freeways were constructed, he drove thousands of miles on the typical two-lane roads of East Texas. Students like Don Benton felt specially privileged when they were chosen to be drivers for President Peeples, or for transporting performers representing Lon Morris College.

In driving across the bounds of the Texas Conference from the Red River to the Gulf of Mexico, Peeples personally recruited many students from parsonage homes of Methodist pastors, as well as those who indicated an interest in pursuing a church-related vocation. In contacts with high schools, he was ready to drive unlimited miles to invite promising students to consider attending Lon Morris College.

The Great Depression was a staggering reality for virtually all prospective students. President Peeples would visit with prospective students and their parents and ask how much they would be able to contribute to the nine months of the next school year. Then he would propose to make up the difference by contacting friends of Lon Morris or pastors, saying, "We have this outstanding young person who is eager to come to Lon Morris, but we must find a way to offer a scholarship of two or three hundred dollars, or he will have to attend the community college close to home, or be denied the opportunity for a college education." Often, that scholarship appeal would be met by twenty dollars from a Sunday school class, or fifty dollars from some lay person who had learned to trust what Cecil Peeples said. Often, a pastor would be given the harsh financial circumstances of an eager, prospective student, with Peeples doing the math in his own handwriting on the bottom of a letter, followed with the question, "Can you help us find one hundred dollars to put this young woman in college? If you can find one hundred dollars, I will find the balance that is needed."

With that great investment in virtually every student who enrolled in Lon Morris, Peeples kept in touch with all that was happening on the campus. He was not timid about reminding students of how many people were counting on them to make good.

Until World War II had brought the Economic Depression to an end, sometimes very creative means were required to finance the meager amounts that students were expected to pay. For instance, occasionally a student might be credited for part of the tuition with the contribution of a milk cow that could become part of the college dairy. One student from Wood

County brought a fine cow that produced an abundance of milk, but was so hard to milk that the students working in the dairy persuaded the business manager of the college to allow them to keep the calves to produce meat for the dinning hall. The ingenious students then allowed the calves to nurse on this hard to milk cow and solved the problem of the hard to milk cow. The father of another student contributed a load of hay to be used by the dairy cows as partial payment on a student's tuition. While the president may not have been personally involved in the operation of the college farm and dairy, all kinds of creative methods were accepted in the Peeples administration to help students meet the demands of financing a college education.

As invitations came from Methodist churches across East Texas to bring a Lon Morris singing group or dramatic group for a visit, Peeples would frequently travel with the students. It was a pleasant trip for the girls' trio to travel in President Peeples' own car, but sometimes a sextet crowded into the single automobile for a two or three hour trip. The relationships that such intimate association produced may help explain why generation after generation of Lon Morris students felt that part of the intangible plus they received from Lon Morris was more than could be measured in academic terms.

Perhaps no other student traveled more with President Peeples than Ruth Alexander. She first knew Dr. Peeples in childhood as he was a regular customer at her father's Sinclair Service Station just half a block from First Methodist Church. While in grade school, she began taking private lessons from Zula Pearson in the drama department at Lon Morris College, so she remarked that she grew up on the college campus. Upon completing high school, she was already part of the Lon Morris community, so she was frequently asked to visit churches along with other students who would provide special music and she was expected to provide some dramatic reading. Sometimes the calls came near bedtime on Saturday night, but Ruth reports that she never declined an opportunity to travel with President Peeples. Some months it seemed to be every Sunday, and at times it would include both Sunday morning and Sunday evening worship.

The most frequent request from Dr. Peeples was for a selection entitled, "The Volunteer Organist" that told the story of the Sunday morning the organist failed to appear, and the congregation was asked if there were anyone present who could play the organ. After an awkward delay, a bleary-eyed old man shuffled to the front, and began to play – and there was music like that congregation had never heard before.

Ruth recalls that she set up the congregation and after that emotional and dramatic buildup, Dr. Peeples always had the congregation completely in hand.

By traveling with students, and sharing in the concerns for selection of those who would be chosen to appear in the dramatic productions and other programs that would represent the college, students felt that it was a very unique experience to have the president of the college take such personal interest in them. Ruth recalls that it was clear that everything was done for Lon Morris, and so students were challenged to do their best for Lon Morris.

After years of teaching in high school and at Centenary College, Ruth Alexander returned to join the faculty at Lon Morris just as Cecil Peeples was preparing to retire. Like so many others, she felt that her life had been especially blessed by the many miles which she had traveled for Lon Morris

College with Cecil Peeples.

Ruth Alexander remembers Dr. Peeples as the eternal optimist: "He woke up every morning with hopeful and optimistic expectations for that day; and he ended every day recounting the good things that had happened and with eager expectations for the new day ahead."

Peeples kept in touch with students beyond graduation. It was natural for him to follow those who considered Lon Morris their first step toward ordained ministry. They would meet at annual conference and in district gatherings, because he never passed an opportunity to represent Lon Morris wherever a Methodist conference might be in session. At one time, more than one hundred of the pastors of the Texas Conference in East Texas were alumni of Lon Morris. These students brought Cecil Peeples' name before the conference when delegates were being chosen for the Jurisdictional Conference, and in 1948 Cecil Peeples was elected.

Those who followed vocations other than the ministry were not forgotten. Especially remarkable were the number of Lon Morris graduates who achieved distinction in the fields of drama and communication arts.

Herbert "Red" Antoine became a senior announcer for NBC.

Sandy Duncan was an East Texas girl who developed special gifts and an outstanding national career in the field of drama. She became a familiar name in television drama and television ads, and starred on Broadway as "Peter Pan." Early in her career she experienced a critical illness from which she lost the vision in one eye; and millions of admirers were inspired by the heroic manner in which she triumphed over that tragedy and continued her outstanding career of national and international fame. Lon Morris proudly claimed her as a former student.

Another performer who achieved national prominence in the entertainment world who was a product of the Lon Morris drama department was Tommy Tune.

Education, law, medicine, public service, and business all had their share of folk who traced the beginning of their preparation for their chosen field to the impact of a small school that was symbolized for nearly four decades by one dynamic leader—Cecil Peeples.

In telling a few of these stories, the risk is recognized and accepted that no doubt the most thrilling stories have not been included. Countless persons with limited resources and limited opportunities were given a vision beyond what anyone could have expected—and most of them would say that Cecil Peeples represented the force and influence that had made the difference in their lives. Across the four decades of this presidency, multiplied hundreds and thousands of hours had been spent by Cecil Peeples literally "on the road for and with students."

Mission statements for colleges and other institutions were not in vogue until the final decades of the twentieth century. But if the question had been raised, "What is the purpose or reason for being for Lon Morris College?" Anyone who knew Cecil Peeples understood that it was clearly for students who, in critical years for crucial decisions, came to expand their horizons and find a sense of direction and purpose for their lives. Simply by the priority he gave to knowing and traveling with students it was clear that Cecil Peeples had a mission and a passion for students, and as faculty members and trustees witnessed his devotion to students, they were ready to share his dreams and support his leadership.

As Peeples began his third year as a college president, the son of an immigrant tenant farmer joined the Lon Morris student body on a football scholarship. The name of Johnny Petrash became legendary as one who typified the spirit of Lon Morris. His family was among a South Texas community of Czech farmers and his accent would always betray the fact that English was not his first language. In his middle teenage years, his father informed him that he had all the education he needed, and that he was now needed to work full time on the farm. Still in the middle of the Great Depression, Johnny Petrash left home and somehow found his way to Victoria Junior College and earned a place on the football squad where boosters encouraged him with assistance in finding odd jobs that would supply resources for food and clothing.

Upon completing high school requirements, somehow he found his way to Lon Morris. Under the Providence of God by means unknown to this writer, he made football his ticket to college. Although much smaller than most college football players, he made up for his lack of size with dogged determination and a keen competitive spirit. Continuing to survive with no financial support beyond his football scholarship and the odd jobs that he had learned to bring out of nowhere, he responded with an overwhelming sense of gratitude for the opportunity of getting a college education. In the public speaking class with Zula Pearson he had one theme for every speech that he made in class: "He Can Who Thinks He Can." In his broken English he convinced other students that "where there is a will there is also a way." Elsewhere in this book the story of the 1938 football miracle victory over Kilgore Junior College is told in which Johnny Petrash scored the winning touchdown.

Upon completing Lon Morris, Petrash went to a state senior college, still playing football; and then he went into service in World War II. He suffered life-threatening injuries and required many months for full recuperation, and then went into a public school teaching career. He married and had a wonderful family, spending the last part of his teaching career in Baytown, Texas, where he was an active member of Grace United Methodist Church. In retirement he spent many hours tending the yard and flower gardens of the church, growing flowers that he shared with neighbors and friends. Petrash was typical of many students who simply would never have had the chance of a college education if Lon Morris had not given that opportunity and then taught them that no obstacle was too great to be overcome.

As Petrash graduated in the spring, one of the students who came that fall from Polk County, the son of a Baptist preacher, also used a football scholarship as a ticket to college. Norris Starkey immediately attracted attention beyond football and was elected president of the Religious Council. As he also prepared for a career in public education, he continued his friendship with another Lon Morris student, Inez Weesner from Frankston, and they were married. They both taught school in small East Texas communities and he moved into school administration and returned to Jacksonville after some years as superintendent of public schools. As a prominent citizen and member of First United Methodist Church in Jacksonville, his friendship with Cecil Peeples continued the relationship from his student days, and eventually they would both be retired in the same community and the same church. At the memorial service upon the death of Cecil Peeples, Norris Starkey was one of the pallbearers.

Consider the story of Billy Tubbs who grew up on the streets of Tulsa, living with an older brother after both parents had died. Upon completing high school, he was not tall enough to be invited to play college basketball, but somehow he heard about Lon Morris and wrote the basketball coach, O.P. Adams. Something about the way Billy Tubbs pursued that relationship prompted an invitation for a tryout, and eventually led to his enrolling at Lon Morris. There he met Pat Ousley, a student from nearby Anderson County, and they would later be married. After completing Lon Morris, he went on to Lamar University in Beaumont where he was recognized for his exceptional drive and determination, and he was retained at Lamar as an assistant coach. Cecil Peeples continued to follow his development, and would have been among those giving his endorsement when Billy Tubbs left Lamar to become head basketball coach at Southwestern University in Georgetown, Texas. After only a brief tenure at Southwestern, Tubbs went on to become head basketball coach at North Texas State University in Denton, and then back to Lamar University as head coach.

In 1980, Tubbs became head basketball coach at Oklahoma University, where he attracted national attention with an exciting and unique style of play from his teams. While at Oklahoma, he suffered a life-threatening injury when he was struck by an automobile while jogging. After months of therapy, he recovered and returned to his coaching duties. While at Oklahoma, his son, Tommy, enrolled at Lon Morris to play basketball; he then returned to Oklahoma University and played on another fine team under his father. In the mid-nineties, Billy Tubbs resigned at Oklahoma to accept the head coaching position for Texas Christian University's basketball program.

How many inspiring stories of students, like that of Billy Tubbs, would trace the decisive turning point in their lives to doors that were opened by Cecil Peeples, or Lon Morris College during the years of the Peeples administration?

Not every student who enrolled in Lon Morris went on to create a Horatio Alger story of success. There were those who found the obstacles too great, others who succumbed to the temptations of compromise or simply unfortunate choices or decisions. But extremely rare was any student in Lon Morris even for a few weeks who did not have some personal relationship with President Peeples. Almost without exception, those students felt that decisive and critical moments of their lives could be traced to the direction and opportunity that had been opened to them symbolized by the strong and inspiring personality of President Peeples, whom they would consider a personal friend across all their years.

Across more than half a century, Cecil Peeples left stirring memories "on the road for and with students."

Chapter Six

Developing Trustee Leadership
by
Walter L. Harris

Who could have imagined the impact of the drive Cecil and Gladys Peeples were making on the morning of June 21, 1935? With courage and fortitude, they made their way north from the Polk County town of Livingston to Jacksonville in Cherokee County. These young partners-in-ministry were well-endowed with the toughness and discipline that growing up on the Great Plains can produce. And here they were, with Cecil preparing to assume the presidency of Lon Morris College during one of the darkest years of the Great Depression, and certainly during a critical period in the history of an institution which had, for many years, been bogged in financial struggle. No doubt some saw their coming to Lon Morris as just another in a long succession of presidents who were appointed, served for a few years, and moved on to another ministerial appointment within the Texas Conference.

Moving day involved an exchange of appointments between H.T. Morgan and Cecil Peeples. The ability of Cecil and Gladys Peeples to turn their appointment into one which lasted thirty-eight years until his retirement in 1973 involved an uncommon measure of faith, vision, and commitment. He was 32, Gladys was 30, and their daughter Nelda was six months old. The birth of their second daughter, Gerri, was still two years in the future The vision which they began to live out on that Summer day in 1935 was profoundly influenced by their earlier experience at Methodist institutions, particularly his at Meridian College, and theirs at Clarendon College and Southern Methodist University. However clear the vision may have been at the start, its articulation along the way was greatly enhanced by the people skills of Cecil Peeples. He understood from the beginning that the only chance for the college's survival and ultimate well-being hinged on a strong and supportive relationship between the president, trustees, the Texas Annual Conference, the Jacksonville business community and the populace generally.

A review of the minutes of the board of trustees from the beginning of the Peeples era to the end of his presidency shows a continuously emerging pattern of positive relationships between trustees and the administration. Board minutes from the 1930s tended to be rather formal with almost no clues as to the full extent of discussion. Sometimes an obviously complex issue was noted in the minutes with a terse one-sentence record of only the outcome. In the written records of the board of trustees, the first clue of the resignation of H.T. Morgan as president came in the minutes of the annual meeting of May 20, 1935. President Morgan made his annual report to the board at that meeting, and at the same time submitted his resignation and request to be relieved of the presidency as soon as possible. The board voted to accept the resignation of Mr. Morgan as soon as his successor could be named.

On June 14, 1935, the board met in a called meeting at 8 a.m. at Texas State Bank in Jacksonville. T.E. Acker, board secretary, made the report of the nominating committee stating that a unanimous nomination of C.E. Peeples for the presidency of Lon Morris College had been reached. What would become an historic selection was recorded with the simple notation, "Motion by Mr. I.T. Shotwell that the nomination of Mr. Peeples be accepted." At the suggestion of Reverend Glenn Flinn, the vote was taken by a written ballot. The ballot count showed eleven votes for and none against C.E. Peeples for the presidency. Board chairman J.C. Beard was instructed to appoint a committee of three to five trustees to work with the new president to develop a plan, "a forward-movement plan," to present to Annual Conference in the fall. Cecil Peeples was called into the meeting, and made a brief statement expressing appreciation to the board, after which Reverend Morgan "made a statement expressing interest [in Lon Morris] and confidence in Mr. Peeples." Seven days later Cecil Peeples assumed the presidency.

The composition of the board of trustees, by the terms of the college's constitution and by-laws in effect in 1935, was evenly divided between lay and clerical members. Generally, lay members tended to be re-nominated and re-elected to the board for successive four-year terms, and clerical members rotated off the board for at least one year following the expiration of their term. The first board vacancy of the Peeples administration came with the death of Senator J.J. Faulk of Athens in the summer of 1935. Senator Faulk had been present at the annual meeting in May, just prior to the election of Cecil Peeples, and had made a strong plea for support of Lon Morris College, citing its importance to Methodism and the Texas Conference. He urged that "we ... support the college," making specific reference to the endowment fund. In his will he made some significant bequests to Lon Morris and to the Conference Board of Superannuate Endowment; and at the death of Mrs. Faulk, a few years later, the endowment fund was a major beneficiary of the J.J. and Gennie Faulk Estates.

At an executive committee meeting in July, 1935, it was suggested that W.R. Nicholson of Longview be nominated to fill the vacancy created by the death of Senator Faulk. Although the committee chose to wait for some degree of outside input before submitting the nomination, Nicholson was ultimately selected as Judge Faulk's successor and served for many years as a trustee.

Geographic board representation of the various areas of the Texas Conference was as much a factor in board member selection as was the lay-clerical composition of the board. Ministers were usually nominated and selected because of their influence in the Conference, the prominence of their appointment, their demonstrated interest in Lon Morris, or because of the anticipation that they could and would assist in reaching some key lay person who was a member of their church. Through his God-given gift of "reading" and relating to people, Cecil Peeples developed a very distinct style of cultivating movers and shakers.

In the earliest years of his presidency, the Peeples board lacked the broad lay representation of the Conference that was later to be achieved. Interestingly enough, there does not appear to be a Houston lay contingent until well after 1935. Tyler, Longview and the East Texas Oil Field were represented early-on by such men as R.W. Fair, W.R. Nicholson, Judge T.D. Campbell, and W.E. Stewart, but it was several years before a major lay presence was evident from the Beaumont-Port Arthur area. H.F. Banker of Port Arthur came on the board in 1945, and Madison Farnsworth and Latimer Murfee were among the first lay members of the Peeples era from Houston.

Peeples recognized and respected the role of Jacksonville

in providing leadership on the board and for the college. The board chairman for almost all of the Peeples tenure was a Jacksonville resident. J.C. Beard served as board chairman from 1924 until his death in 1937. A respected Jacksonville business man, Beard was a partner with I.T. Shotwell and T.E. Acker in Jacksonville Grain and Commission Company. Although he lived only two years into the Peeples administration, his son-in-law T.E. Acker was elected to the chairmanship to succeed Beard, and served in that capacity from 1937 until his death in 1972. On assuming the chairmanship Acker was already an 18-year veteran of the Lon Morris Board, having served as its secretary since 1919.

A Jacksonville banker, merchant, thirty-three year mayor, and prominent Methodist layman, Acker had a major influence on the history of Lon Morris College from as early as 1919 and for well over half a century. "Mr.Tom" was a perennial delegate to Annual Conferences, Jurisdictional Conferences, and General Conferences of the Methodist Church through all the middle years of the twentieth century. From the 1930s until shortly before his death in 1972, Mr. Tom was the teacher of the Men's Wesley Bible Class in Jacksonville's First Methodist Church, and for many of those years his morning Sunday School lesson was broadcast around the Jacksonville area by radio station KEBE.

The relationship between the College and Jacksonville's First Methodist Church has been both historic and a matter of record written into the College's by-laws. During the Peeples era the ministers of First Methodist included L.W. Nichols, Sr., Neal Cannon, Stewart Clendenin, Marvin Vance, Jack Sparling, Don Peavey, Carlos Davis, Robert Langham, James Heflin, Ernest Phifer, and Robert Gilpin. Each of these men, along with the district superintendents of the Jacksonville District, and its successor the Palestine District served ably in an ex-officio capacity as members of the board and of the executive committee. Several of these ministers served as board members after leaving their pastoral ministry at First Methodist Church.

L.W. Nichols, Sr., who was minister at the time of Cecil Peeples' election was a contributing member of the board much of the time throughout the remaining active years of his ministry. His son Talley W. Nichols, who became the father of modern manufacturing in Jacksonville, was a dedicated and effective lay member of the board from the 1950s well into the 1980s, and Talley's tenure on the board was followed by that of his son Robert L. Nichols, who remains a board member today.

One of the longest-tenured board members of the Peeples presidency was W. Glenn Goodwin who was elected to the board in 1937, and who served continuously, most of the time as board secretary, until the time of his death in 1970. Goodwin was a Methodist layman of prominence, and a dedicated servant of Lon Morris College. He was the local manager of the 3 Beall Brothers 3 store in Jacksonville, and served First Methodist Church of Jacksonville in a wide variety of capacities.

It was I.T. Shotwell who made the motion to elect Cecil Peeples as president in 1935, and Shotwell remained a member of the executive committee until he moved to Littlefield, Texas. Even then, his interest in the college, his participation in its affairs, and his friendship and correspondence with Cecil Peeples continued. With very few exceptions, Shotwell made the trip back to Jacksonville for annual board meetings.

Not only did Peeples cherish the relationship between the

College and First Methodist Church, but also he was a frequent visitor to other churches in Jacksonville. Even though Peeples usually was on the road preaching, telling the Lon Morris story, and raising funds at Methodist churches outside Jacksonville on Sunday mornings, he and Mrs. Peeples almost always worshipped together in Jacksonville on Sunday nights, no matter how far he had driven to arrive at home in time for evening services.

Ruth Alexander tells the story of one particular trip out with Dr. Peeples on a day that those whose memory goes back to the World War II era will always remember.

She says, "On December 7, 1941, Brother Peeples, Evelyn Walters, and I went to Normangee for the morning church services. We had lunch at the parsonage and started home. We came through Crockett to pick up Miss Thelma Martensen, and continued to Jacksonville. Since the other three lived on campus they took me to my dad's service station (in those days no service station closed on Sunday). My dad ran out yelling, 'I'm joining the army—the Japanese have attacked Pearl Harbor!' We had been happily driving through the country for two hours with not an inkling of the historic date the day had become.

"Brother Peeples had a radio brought to the auditorium on the second floor of the Twin Towers building, [on Monday Morning] and we all went there to hear Franklin Roosevelt ask Congress to declare war on the Japanese Empire. Lives changed forever!"

Through the years Peeples developed many local friendships outside the Methodist Church, and in fact made it a point to cultivate community-wide support through involvement in civic work and through visiting and sometimes preaching in other churches in Jacksonville. One highly effective trustee was W.W. Holman, a Baptist layman and member of Central Baptist Church in Jacksonville. Holman, a consistent Lon Morris supporter and booster, was proprietor of Cobb-Holman Lumber Company in Jacksonville. His potential as a board member was not lost on Cecil Peeples as the college began to enter the bricks and mortar period which characterized the fifties, sixties, and seventies. He was far more than, as he called himself, "the token Baptist on the board." Holman was a friend of the college and of Cecil Peeples through the years; and his children, many of his grandchildren and some of their spouses attended Lon Morris College.

A Jacksonville board member who served a unique but highly essential role on the board was Ernest Odom. A Methodist layman, Odom was partner in Williamson-Odom Furniture Company of Jacksonville. His counsel, discounts, creative financing, and genuine concern for the future of Lon Morris made him a valuable member.

When Talley Nichols moved his toy pistol manufacturing plant to Jacksonville in the mid-fifties, it did not take Cecil Peeples long to enlist Nichols' talent in the Lon Morris effort. Son of a Methodist minister, and brother of another, Nichols caught the Peeples vision for the future of the college and has demonstrated ongoing generosity for Lon Morris causes through the years. During the sixties when his business interests were extremely demanding of his personal time and energy, Nichols found time to participate in the business of the college, even to the extent of making the drive to Houston with fellow trustees for major board meetings. On one of these occasions he confided to several others on the trip that there were only three people in Jacksonville whom he did not feel comfortable in calling by their first name: "Mr. Tom" Acker, "Mr. Gus" Blankenship, and Dr. Peeples.

Cecil Peeples was a man of absolute integrity. From time to time board members would do thoughtful things for Peeples, sometimes of monetary value, as a token of their admiration and respect for the man and the quality of his work. It was almost impossible to bring about such an intent without precipitating a gift to Lon Morris College along the way. Once or twice a year Madison Farnsworth would call or write Dr. Peeples and ask him to go by Leopold, Price and Rolle (a fashionable men's store) the next time he was in Houston to pick out a new suit. It was always navy blue, always a high quality suit, and always an event that triggered a gift from Cecil Peeples to Lon Morris College. Dr. Peeples would come into the business office and say, "Madison wanted me to get this suit, and it is more expensive than what I would have paid on my own, so receipt this check to the scholarship fund in honor of Madison Farnsworth." If it were a $300 suit, Dr. Peeples would probably make a gift to the college of $100 or $150.

Because of the respect and affection Peeples enjoyed on the Jacksonville scene, businesses sometimes gave him discounts on personal purchases. For many years he used the services of Young Cleaners, operated by Homer and Lorene Ragsdale. When his personal cleaning bill would come, it carried a 50% discount. If the bill for the month was $45, he would write a personal check to Young Cleaners for $22.50, and he would write another check of the same amount to Lon Morris College for either the scholarship or living endowment fund. These discount amounts were receipted to Young

Cleaners, and the receipt was sent with his personal thank you letter every month for many years.

Ed Kiely, a former Lon Morris student and longtime Jacksonville printer, recalls how Peeples possessed the art of expressing genuine gratitude for small acts. "When I was just getting my printing business started," Kiely recalls, "I carried Dr. Peeples two boxes of envelopes, and maybe some letterheads just as a token of appreciation and support. You would have thought that I gave him a thousand dollars. He knew how to make you feel important to the college." Marvin Vance remarked at a Peeples appreciation banquet in 1958 that "Cecil Peeples possesses an ability to be as genuinely appreciative of a five dollar gift as he is for five thousand dollars." Peeples was almost always successful in acknowledging a gift of either size in a special and personal way.

So much of the story of Cecil Peeples' trustee relationships revolves around events which developed over time in the Southeast Texas area! The Houston-Beaumont-Port Arthur and Galveston areas loomed large in the history of LMC after 1940. It is probably more than coincidence that the building of strong lay leadership on the board from these areas occurred in tandem with the membership and involvement of Bishop A. Frank Smith on the Lon Morris Board. Bishop Smith was made an ex officio member in 1943, and board meetings tended to be scheduled to accommodate his calendar, whether in Jacksonville or in Houston. Where the bishop went, there often followed ministers who wanted to be involved, and if one minister brought along an influential layman who had great potential in the college's future there was likely to be an idea born in the mind of another. It may not have been planned that way, but that is how it worked; and

Cecil Peeples knew how to use the situation to the advantage of Lon Morris College.

There was a special bond between Peeples and H.F. Banker of Port Arthur. Banker, a Port Arthur businessman, had been prominent in the work of the Beaumont District of The Methodist Church in the early thirties while the Peeples were serving in Wiergate. He would later serve as the Conference Lay Leader, a position which afforded him an effective forum for support of LMC causes. The acquaintance and friendship established at that time bore fruit for Lon Morris in the immediate post World War II period. Banker became a Lon Morris board member in 1945, and attended his first board meeting just days after "V-E Day" in May of that year. He quickly demonstrated his interest in improving the condition of, and expanding, the physical plant, and he proved his commitment consistently throughout the future years of his service on the board. Banker was chairman of the Building Committee up to the time when he had to retire for reasons of health, and was highly influential in getting the Fine Arts Building started. He, along with Windmill Phillips and R.W. Fair, came to the defense of the Peeples presidency with vigor and persuasiveness when one faction within the Texas Conference applied pressure for Peeples' replacement in late 1952 and the spring of 1953. Out of this incident there emerged a renewed and motivated administration that moved onward and upward for the next twenty years.

One of the most effective Houston lay board members was Madison Farnsworth. Farnsworth was a member of St. Paul's Methodist Church and was a highly placed regional executive of Gulf Oil Corporation. He joined the Lon Morris board early in 1952, and demonstrated his effectiveness from the beginning in the area of promoting scholarship funding. Farnsworth was by no means a single-interest board member, however, and his promotion of endowment growth and his support of the building effort are well-documented.

Madison Farnsworth may have made his most memorable contribution to the college when he helped bring about the involvement of Eddy C. Scurlock as a board member. Scurlock, by the early fifties, was fast becoming one of the most recognized names in the oil industry in Houston. He was a charter member of St. Luke's Methodist Church in Houston's River Oaks and had played a major role in the building of that church in the 1940s. Scurlock's first project in support of the college was the relatively modest provision of new robes for the college choir. Both Peeples and Farnsworth saw a far greater potential in Scurlock, and were able to use the influence of his minister, Dr. Durwood Fleming, to steer him toward board membership. Scurlock first attended a board meeting on October 31, 1952, at Gregg County Airport in Longview. At that meeting Dr. Peeples presented several matters pertaining to the building of the proposed fine arts building. Even though it was his first meeting, Scurlock proposed that the planned new building be named in honor of Bishop A. Frank Smith. The motion was seconded by Walter Fair and carried unanimously. Lon Morris board meetings would never be quite the same again!

Less than three months later, in January 1953, the executive committee of the board met for the purpose of letting the contract for the building. Arthur Thompson, a retired Jacksonville builder, was employed to begin the building. For the next decade, until the completion of the Simon and Louise Henderson Library and the Jimmie Owen Administration

Building, Thompson was a key player with Peeples and the board as a new physical plant was built. His arrangement with the college was that of a construction manager. Although his work was done on a "cost-plus" basis, Thompson enjoyed great credibility with Peeples, the building committee, and the board.

In the spring of 1959, H.F. Banker resigned from the board for health reasons, but his service to the college, particularly as chairman of the building committee, earned him the designation of honorary board member for life. He was replaced as chairman of the building committee by E.C. Scurlock, who was already a member of that committee, and W.A. "Abe" Pounds was named to the committee to fill the vacancy. Pounds was the Tyler banker who provided the line of credit necessary for the building program to proceed, and he was also the treasurer of the Texas Annual Conference. A widowed sister of Pounds, Mrs. D.S. (Lena) Hotchkiss, was a longtime dorm mother, first at Lula Morris Hall and later at Fair Hall, and was a deeply loved and respected member of the college staff. Her relationship with the college extended well into the 1960s when she remarried and moved to El Paso.

Also in 1959 Simon W. Henderson of Lufkin was named to the board. By this time the board membership included Jimmie Owen, formerly of Overton and now an independent oilman from Lafayette, Louisiana. At first, Henderson's and Owen's interest and influence were mainly in the area of the building program. Very shortly, they became the benefactors of the Simon and Louise Henderson Library and the Jimmie Owen Administration Building.

Another trustee whose influence grew in the late fifties was Arnold Reed. Reed, a 1935 graduate of LMC, lived in

95

Little Rock, Arkansas earlier in the decade, and achieved substantial success in the life insurance business. In the mid-fifties, he moved to Dallas and founded Great Commonwealth Life Insurance Company, Inc. While still in Arkansas, he made a strong appeal for businesses "to put Lon Morris College on their payroll," a call to which he personally responded with a $500 monthly gift. This was the beginning of the "living endowment program." On the board of trustees, Reed demonstrated interest in improving faculty housing, an influence that was deeply appreciated by the faculty. He was also a prime mover in the organization of the Board of Development, a training place for future trustees, and he served as its first chairman. This board raised thousands of dollars for a wide range of special projects.

In early 1961 the College was fully apprised of the statewide campaign and organization of "United Capital Funds Inc. for Texas Methodist Colleges." By this time the resident bishop of the Texas Annual Conference was Bishop Paul Martin, who was extremely supportive of Methodist-related higher education, and who attended and participated in Lon Morris board meetings with regularity and great effectiveness. The executive director of the United Capital Funds campaign was Charles Musgrove. Although he was never a board member, he became a major participant in LMC board meetings through all the remaining years of the Peeples administration. When the United Capital Funds campaign was concluded, Musgrove stayed in close connection with the college through his new role of chief administrator of the Texas Methodist College Association. The general chairman of the United Capital Funds was R.E. "Bob" Smith, one of Houston's best known independent oil operators, and a member of

Houston's First Methodist Church. Smith, along with his new minister Dr. Charles L. Allen, began to attend board meetings that were held in Houston, and made several trips to Jacksonville to participate in board meetings on the campus.

Beginning sometime in the early sixties, board attendance by the Houston delegation was facilitated by the availability of the Scurlock Oil Company plane. Eddy Scurlock took great delight in being able to bring along ten or fifteen trustees from Houston in his Beechcraft King-Air. The typical delegation often included Bishop Martin, Scurlock, Madison Farnsworth, Latimer Murfee, Arthur Wilson, Joe Cook, J. Kenneth Shamblin, Charles Williams, and Charles L. Allen. Scurlock would usually call just prior to takeoff at Hobby Airport, with instructions to have transportation available at Cherokee County Airport in 45-minutes. Almost like clockwork the plane would appear on the distant southern horizon. It would land, and following a hasty exchange of greetings, the seven-mile ride into Jacksonville would begin another history-making day in the life of Lon Morris College. Wyman Fisher, Virgil Matthews, and I, (Walter Harris) were typically designated to transport the guests to the College.

I recall what is easily the most touching and emotional of these flights, and it did not involve a board meeting, at least not directly.

In late July of 1967, Dr. Peeples went into Nan Travis Hospital in Jacksonville with what he thought were insignificant symptoms, and within a day or two he had been diagnosed as a cancer patient with a condition that might require extensive surgery. Mrs. Peeples asked me to "let Mr. Tom [Acker] know that Peeples will be having surgery in a day or two, and that he might have to be out of the office for a while."

As I told Mr. Tom what was happening, he and I were thinking the same thing. Dr. Peeples should probably go to Houston. At that point, he placed a call to Eddy Scurlock, and told him of the diagnosis. Mr. Scurlock's response was swift and predictable. He said that he would make arrangements at Methodist Hospital for Peeples to be admitted; that the surgery would be done there; and that the Scurlock plane would be standing by to be at Cherokee County Airport on about an hour's notice. Within less than twenty-four hours, Peeples was admitted to Methodist Hospital, and on August 4, 1967, one day before his sixty-fifth birthday, Peeples underwent a seven-hour operation, after which his surgeon, Dr. Stalen, told Mrs. Peeples, "It all went very well, Mrs. Peeples. Your husband is cured of cancer. He will need to be shot when he's about ninety."

When Dr. Peeples was able to leave the hospital, the Scurlocks insisted that he come out to their River Oaks home where he and Mrs. Peeples would be house guests for a few weeks. The Peeples spent about three weeks there, and when the Scurlock plane landed back at Cherokee County Airport in early September, there were tears of joy and thanksgiving. Tom Acker, Barnes H. Broiles, Wyman Fisher, and I were there to greet them, and there were no dry eyes among us! It was a memorable experience.

The school years 1960-1961 and 1961-1962 involved a great new surge of trustee influence and involvement. With the United Capital Funds campaign well underway, and with the Twin Towers having been razed in the fall of 1960, the opportunity for board members to assert leadership was everywhere. Jimmie Owen had made a commitment to pay for the new Administration Building, and the Simon Henderson family was providing the new Simon and Louise Henderson Library through the Simon and Louise Henderson Foundation. Their procedure in the making of their gift was to provide monthly checks in the amount of whatever the construction cost for the month had been. The library building was fully paid for on its completion, and it did not involve any debt. When Jimmie Owen made his commitment to build the Administration Building, he started regular monthly payments of $2,000, and from time to time he made additional payments to lower the balance due on his pledge. The total cost of the administration building was about $112,000 excluding furnishings.

One of the most exciting board meetings of the whole Peeples era was at the Houston Club Building on April 2, 1963. By this time the new library and administration building were completed, and Jimmie Owen had paid a major part of his pledge for the Owen Building's construction. Owen took the floor at the meeting and entertained the board with reminiscences about the highs and lows of the oil business. He ended by saying that he had just sold a substantial part of his oil interests, had paid a lot of debts, and was now prepared to pay off the balance of his pledge on the Jimmie Owen Administration Building. "Walter," he said, "if you'll go over to the Bank of the Southwest at the break and get a blank bank draft, I'll give Lon Morris a check for whatever is owed on my pledge plus a little extra." Harris recalls that when the board broke for coffee "I ran so fast that I got slowed down by a security officer in the bank, and I barely avoided an encounter with the Houston Police when I left the bank. It is not a good thing to run out of banks in big cities." Jimmie Owen wrote a check for about $50,000 to the college, and the next day the Administration Building note was paid in full at Tyler Bank and Trust Company.

The significance of Paul H. Pewitt in the success of the Cecil Peeples presidency cannot be over-stated. Pewitt had been recruited onto the board when he lived in Omaha in the Texarkana District, and he had an instant rapport with Peeples. Initially his support was directed to the scholarship fund, and he "adopted" two or three students each year for whom he paid most expenses subject to their satisfactory performance in their "work-scholarship" assignment. Pewitt was a quiet man, somewhat shy and with a desire to be inconspicuous, but he had a generous heart and spirit. He joined with Eddy Scurlock, Walter Fair, H.F. Banker, Latimer Murfee, Madison Farnsworth, and other major benefactors to advance the cause of the building fund in gifts of $25,000 at a time. The Paul Pewitt Science Building was named in his honor when it was built in 1961. Despite his major contributions to the building program, Pewitt never allowed his interest in the scholarship program to wane. Pewitt's personal will provided a bequest to Lon Morris which was the largest single gift ever received by the college.

The history of the college and of Peeples board relationships in the middle and late-1960s involved names of new members such as Arthur Moore, of Metairie, Louisiana who retired in the Waco area; Carl N. Williford of Fairfield; C.C. Kelley of Beaumont; Gil Phares of Port Arthur; Travis Ward of Athens and Dallas; George W. Pearson of Alvin; R.A. Shepherd and Joe B. Cook of Houston, John W. Ford of Kilgore; and R.G. Beall and James H. Rounsaville of Jacksonville. This period saw the beginning of board membership and influence by Arthur R. Wilson of Houston, who along with his

100

wife, Evie Jo Wilson, provided the gift of the Craven-Wilson Women's Building just as Peeples was retiring. All were active lay-persons who were attracted to the Lon Morris effort by Peeples' commitment to and communication of his vision for the college's future.

Chapter Seven

A New Campus Emerges
by
Walter L. Harris

The Lon Morris campus of 1935 showed the cumulative effect of more than twenty-five years of insufficient resources and maintenance. Deferred maintenance was the rule in many areas of institutional and personal life during the Great Depression, and Lon Morris College was certainly no exception. As the financial situation of the college slowly improved over the years, Cecil Peeples was fond of quoting the counsel offered by former president W.K. Strother who told him to "keep a foundation under it, a roof over it, and the rest can wait." While there is not a lot of evidence of foundation problems, the task of coping with leaking roofs proved to be a considerable challenge in itself.

It would be many years before the college would have any type of full-time maintenance department, and during the first two decades of the Peeples presidency, the upkeep of buildings and grounds was largely in the hands of a designated faculty member such as Arch Pearson, assisted by custodians George Moore, Jack Walker, and others. Student labor was always a significant factor in the maintenance of the college plant, and the work scholarship was an institution that made a college education a possibility for literally thousands of Lon Morris students over the years. Occasionally a student would complain that what they thought was a scholarship turned out to be a job that demanded both time and labor, but most students left Lon Morris with lasting gratitude to Cecil Peeples and the opportunity that work scholarships provided.

The focal point and centerpiece of the Lon Morris campus was the main building known far and wide as the "Twin Towers." The three-story masonry building, constructed in the early twentieth century soon after Lon Morris moved from Kilgore to Jacksonville, was a beautiful, if inefficient, structure that offered a continuing challenge to all who attempted to maintain and work within it. The building contained only six general purpose classrooms, one science classroom with limited laboratory facilities, and the Alexander Library. The six classrooms were situated at the north and south ends of each of the three floors of the building, and the science facility was located on the first floor on the back side of the building.

The center-front portion of the building was devoted to the library on the ground floor, and to administrative offices on the second floor. Most of the second floor consisted of the college auditorium, the ceiling of which extended all the way to the roof of the building. The auditorium balcony was entered from the third floor, which also housed very limited faculty offices and music practice rooms. In the basement of the building there was the boiler room, the source of steam heat for the Twin Towers, London Hall, and Lula Morris Hall.

The Twin Towers had been erected in times of great financial struggle during the first decade of the twentieth century, and although it was razed in 1960 as an early and essential step in the ultimate provision of a modern and efficient physical plant, it remains in the memory of many as the icon of choice insofar as physical facilities are concerned. Built during the presidency of W.K. Strother, the building had cost far more than originally predicted when first proposed. In his 1973 study of the history of Lon Morris College, *Mid the Pine Hills of East Texas,* Glendell A. Jones Jr. describes the College's early twentieth century financial situation as follows:

In 1908-1909, Strother persuaded his trustees to borrow $30,000 in short-term loans to facilitate completion of the Twin Towers building in the hope that the Texas Conference would eventually raise sufficient funds to pay off the building debt. Attempting to reduce his construction costs as much as possible, Strother economized by purchasing building stone of unequal size and by eliminating both front porches and an elevator for the Twin Towers, only to buy a $1,300 piano for the music department. By the spring of 1909 he had spent the entire $30,000 borrowed by his trustees and had to sell the old Sunset Institute property to raise the final $10,000 needed to complete the Twin Towers. At the end of the 1908-1909 session, he tore down the eighteen-year-old institute building and sold its building materials, land, and two frame classroom buildings, which later became the local Episcopal Church and parsonage. With the proceeds of the old property, Strother completed the Twin Towers for a final cost of $60,000, three times his original estimate, in time for the 1909-1910 session, declaring that it "would meet the needs of the school for many years to come."

The building did, indeed, meet the needs of the school for half a century, but a succession of events that had begun with the Panic of 1907, followed by fire, World War I, and the Great Depression that began with the stock market crash of 1929 all combined to provide a thirty-eight year challenge for Cecil Peeples and the Texas Conference of the Methodist Church. As the years passed and old debts were paid, Peeples, his board, his faculty, his students, and Texas Conference Methodism became so involved in the successes of the institution that there was very little time for self-pity. Of course times were hard; certainly there were never enough resources. Not every committee appointed accomplished its purpose, nor did every campaign launched achieve its goal, but the vision of Cecil Peeples was always directed toward the expectation of a brighter tomorrow and, ultimately, toward the achievement of a financial status which could undergird the future of the college for decades to come.

There was little mention of the physical plant in the board minutes during the early Peeples years. At an executive committee meeting late in 1938, T.E. Acker reported that a conference-wide program had been authorized by the Texas Conference to solicit one hundred "$25 Club" members and one thousand "$10 Club" members with debt retirement as the end use of the funds raised. Until the debt inherited from prior administrations was paid and the accumulated accounts payable to local and area merchants could be put out of the way, there just wasn't much incentive to pursue a vigorous program of building or plant expansion.

Peeples was at ease and highly effective in the Jacksonville social and civic environment. In the early years of his presidency he worked closely with local merchant creditors whose dedication to Jacksonville did much to keep the college afloat through the Great Depression. Some months he could make no more than a tiny dent in the mountain of debt he had inherited when he arrived in 1935, but he tried to pay something every month to everybody who was a creditor. This practice endeared him to the business community, and it served him well when it came time to launch and execute major campaigns for building and other capital purposes. He visited churches all over town, and probably did as much to cultivate generous principles of stewardship as any minister who ever served in the pulpit of any Jacksonville church.

The importance of positive relationships with the press was not lost on Cecil Peeples. Through all of his years in the presidency, Peeples treasured the friendship and respect of Raymond "Doc" West, who was editor of the Jacksonville *Daily Progress* until the early 1950s. West and his wife, Fredna, were constant in their support of Lon Morris causes long after they retired from the newspaper business.

When West sold the newspaper, Peeples was quick to cultivate a new and rewarding friendship. Although Cecil Peeples and the new publisher, Barnes H. Broiles, were generally poles apart when it came to national political matters, they were united in their love of Jacksonville and its causes and institutions. Both men involved themselves in civic causes with seemingly limitless energy, and a lasting and effective friendship was formed. They met two or three times a week for coffee, community chat, and the sharing of a developing vision for Jacksonville. Peeples confided in a close associate that "Mr. Broiles and I probably cancel each other's vote every time we go to the polls in state and national elections, but he is one of my best friends. If it's good for Jacksonville or for Lon Morris, he's for it!"

Before 1939, College Avenue was unpaved. In the spring of 1939, Peeples recommended that $700 of College Day funds be used to pave the eight hundred block of College Avenue from Devereaux Street to Prather Street. This was the center of the campus, and the site of the Twin Towers. The work on this one block was accomplished, but it was several years later before Devereaux Street was paved, and 1964 when Prather Street was paved.

One of the first board discussions of the college's needs for permanent facilities expansion came in early 1940. President Peeples explained the necessity for certain improvements to meet minimum accreditation requirements of the Southern Association of Colleges and Secondary Schools. Toward that end, the president recommended an expenditure of $5,400 from the 1940 College Day Offering.

It must be understood that much of the work and planning of Cecil Peeples during the first five years of his administration was directed toward the time when improved facilities would become a reality. As early as 1936, the president presented a plan that incorporated two forward-looking goals: 1) something to do immediately for Lon Morris; and 2) a "higher program" for four or five years in the future. For the immediate objective, Peeples urged a plan for obtaining 100 scholarships of $90 each. On a longer range view, the president asked his board and the Texas Annual Conference to adopt a $250,000 goal for the next five years, with $60,000 to be allocated to debt retirement; $90,000 for buildings and maintenance; and $100,000 for endowment. To those who understood the mind and fiscal philosophy of Cecil Peeples, it is not surprising that his endowment emphasis as laid out in

108

1936 was the largest of the three areas of allocation proposed.

During the 1941-1942 school year, particularly during the fall of 1941, there were references in the board minutes to construction at the college farm, and some evidence of improving financial conditions. Interestingly though, at an executive committee meeting on December 16, 1941, and on February 7, 1942, there was absolutely no reference to World War II or to Pearl Harbor.

At the board's annual meeting of May, 1942, it was proposed that the resident bishop be made an ex-officio member of the board of trustees. Perhaps more than anything else, that act heightened the awareness of the conference of the Lon Morris story, and increased church participation in its programs. It was no accident that the fortunes of the college, both in terms of relationships with individual trustees and with the churches of the Texas Annual Conference, began to improve in a major way with the involvement of Bishop A. Frank Smith in the planning process.

The great building program that began with the construction of the A. Frank Smith Fine Arts Building in 1953 became a defining characteristic of the Peeples administration for the next twenty years.

As the difficulties of the Great Depression were eclipsed by the war years through the first half of the 1940s, it was apparent that the price of more unavoidable deferred maintenance would be major new construction. Between 1946 and 1953, the board began to exert increasing pressure to get something started in the way of a new Fine Arts Building and other construction. On more than one occasion during these years some trustee would initiate pressure to begin construction either of a Fine Arts Building, renovation of the Twin Towers, or for some other purpose. One or more board members would propose the beginning of construction "as soon as possible." What Cecil Peeples understood was that to begin construction without an adequate financial plan in place was to compound the grief and insecurity that had followed the completion of the Twin Towers forty years earlier. It was Peeples' staunch fiscal conservatism that delayed the launching of the building program of the fifties and sixties until he had his "ducks in a row."

Cecil Peeples had great faith and vision, but so much of the power of his vision lay in his understanding of the necessity to have a viable financial plan in place. He knew all too well that a premature decision could recreate the atmosphere of extreme austerity from which the college of the late 1940s and early 1950s was, for the first time in its history, emerging. This man was never opposed to the concept of launching a building program, but he had not the slightest intention of launching or administering a construction effort that was doomed from the beginning by inadequate resources. Fortunately, his patience and persistence paid big and continuing dividends in the twenty years following 1952.

October 31, 1952, was a watershed day in the life of Lon Morris College, particularly of its building program. The board met that day in a fly-in meeting at Gregg County Airport in Longview. Those present included T.E. Acker, W. Glenn Goodwin, Homer Fort, W.R. Swain, R.C. Terry, Joe Z Tower, A.D. Lemons, A.C. Bell, Emmett Dubberly, Dawson Bryan, Dunbar Chambers, Madison Farnsworth, R.W. Fair, W.E. Stewart, H.F. Banker, J. Marcus Wood, J.E. Brown, Eddy C. Scurlock and C.E. Peeples. It was the first board meeting attended by Scurlock, and his influence was felt instantly, initiating a new era in the effort to launch construction of a Fine Arts Building. The meeting produced a decision to pursue immediate construction of a Fine Arts Building, and Eddy Scurlock proposed that the building be named in honor of Bishop A. Frank Smith.

Scurlock exhibited a personal quality that day that would be characteristic of his leadership style and his often-demonstrated habit of giving credit to others. He offered a motion that the citizens of Jacksonville and the Jacksonville Chamber of Commerce be thanked for "the role they have played in raising money for the Fine Arts Building." It was less than three months later, in early 1953, when the executive committee of the board met and employed Arthur Thompson, a semi-retired building contractor, to begin construction of the new building.

The only remaining hurdle to the acceleration of what would become a twenty-year adventure in bricks, mortar, and the cultivation of philanthropy presented itself early in 1953, and was overcome and resolved in a manner that gave Cecil Peeples unprecedented prestige and respect among Methodists of the Texas Annual Conference for the remainder of his presidential tenure.

The thirty-eight years of the Peeples presidency spanned a period of national history from the depths of the Great Depression to the unfolding of the Watergate fiasco that brought down a president of the United States. World War II, the Korean War, the Vietnam War, the popularization of television as a communications and entertainment medium, the coming of jet flight as a favored means of commercial travel, and the actual landing of man's first flight to the moon all fell within the time frame of the approximately 14,000 days which were his presidency.

Peeples' task as president was never without struggle, but the struggle was bearable because he possessed the consistency of faith, vision, and purpose that he lived out so magnificently. His tolerance for struggle was no doubt enhanced by his unwavering personal integrity. There were no scandals in the Peeples administration.

Only once during Peeples' lengthy presidential tenure was the security of his appointment as president threatened. Strangely enough, the issue of the launching of the building program that began in 1953 was at least a factor in the threat. Some of the preachers in the Texas Conference felt that the start of the Fine Arts Building construction had been too-long delayed. Others perceived the future of the college as too tenuous to justify a major building program, and there was a real and very present question about how the Texas Conference support of the college would continue in the face of major and growing expectations for support of Lakeview Methodist Assembly near Palestine. There was a feeling on the part of some that the time to close Lon Morris was at hand. At a meeting in May of 1953 the issue came to a head, and it was ultimately resolved in a manner that placed Cecil Peeples in a stronger position than he had ever enjoyed before.

The trustees met in a special called session at Marvin Methodist Church in Tyler on May 14, 1953. Cecil Peeples asked and was granted permission to make an "uninterrupted report" and retired from the meeting room. T.E. Acker made a statement to clarify the reason for the special called meeting, which was to take the place of a regular meeting originally scheduled for May 25. He stated that full discussion of the program of Lon Morris College, its needs and its future, should be put before the whole board in order to establish unity among board members and "thereby to stop adverse rumors concerning the College."

This, the most tense of all Peeples-era meetings, was apparently as much about closing the college as it was about the start of a building program or the hiring of a new president. A motion by A.D. Lemons, seconded by Dawson Bryan, was passed, calling for the chairman to bring in a recommendation for the hiring of a new president. The committee, charged with submitting its report at 10 a.m. on June 1 in Houston, consisted of Homer Fort, chairman, Guy H. Wilson, Dawson Bryan, H.F. Banker, and Dunbar Chambers.

H.F. Banker, Wallace A. Phillips, Walter Fair and Dunbar Chambers rose to Peeples' defense immediately at the May 14 meeting, but a final disposition of the issue had to wait until the June 1 Houston meeting.

At the Houston meeting two and a half weeks later, the committee made its report with the recommendation that 1) Cecil Peeples be elected Lon Morris College president for the 1953-1954 year; 2) a program and policy committee give thorough study to the policies of, and an adequate program for, the College; and that the Executive Committee be enlarged by addition of four persons: two ministers and two laymen, subject to approval of the board and of the Annual Conference. The proposed program and policy committee was appointed to include Dunbar Chambers, Stewart Clendenin, Dawson Bryan, H.F. Banker, Walter Fair, and Joe Z Tower.

The crisis had passed. Construction of the A. Frank Smith Fine Arts Building continued. Cecil Peeples salary was raised, and never again was his appointment as president of Lon Morris College threatened or insecure. Nor would the College

113

close! By early the next year the Fine Arts Building was nearing completion, and the board was profuse in its praise of the work being done by Cecil Peeples, Arthur Thompson, Tom Acker and others. On at least one occasion Bishop Smith likened the meetings of the Lon Morris College Board to meetings of the "mutual admiration society."

By November of 1954 the Executive Committee was pursuing the question of the best use of the auditorium of the Twin Towers Building. There was some discussion of the possibility of converting the Twin Towers auditorium into a library, and in turn converting the ground-floor library into administrative offices. The trustees even went so far as to engage the services of S.W. Ray for study of the architectural modifications that these changes would involve, and to discuss with Arthur Thompson the probable cost of the actual work being considered. Within a month it received a recommendation from architect S.W. Ray that the building be razed and replaced with a modern fireproof building.

The more immediate interest, however, was in getting construction started on a new dormitory for women. At the October 1954 meeting, Guy H. Wilson called for an exploration by the building committee of the possibilities for a new dormitory, and at a board meeting in March, 1955, H.F. Banker and E.C. Scurlock called for the start of such a building "sometime this fall." By August the board authorized the necessary borrowing to build and furnish a new dormitory for women. By the May meeting in 1956, the building committee was preparing to borrow the final $150,000 needed to finish the project, and was looking well beyond to the next round of needed facilities additions.

The meeting of May 21, 1956, brought the adoption of a

18.
Gerri and Nelda
Peeples are in
front of the
President's Home
at 617 College
Avenue. 1954

Courtesy of
Gladys Peeples

115

$4,000,000 long-range program to include $1.5 million for endowment and endowed lectureships, and physical additions and improvements including a dining hall, student center, academic center, classrooms, science laboratories, administrative offices, chapel, overhaul of men's dormitories, and provision for several faculty homes and apartments.

By early 1957 Eddy Scurlock had really asserted his leadership role on the board. It was at that time that he set off serious discussion of the proposed addition of a new student center and dining hall on the campus. It was his proposal, seconded by H.F. Banker on February 21, 1957, that authorized the removal of the Bolin Home from the corner of College and Devereaux Streets. This would become the future site of the E.C. Scurlock Student Center, although the exact name of the center was far less important to Scurlock than the obvious need for its existence. In fact, it was not until the meeting of February 21, 1957, that the recently-completed women's dormitory was officially named. Upon motion of H.F. Banker, seconded by John Wesley Hardt, the new dormitory was named in honor of R.W. Fair, and in memory of Mrs. R.W. Fair.

In a major meeting of the board in April, 1958, the board, through its building committee, presented a "Challenge to the Conference" for the decade of the 1960s. The challenge called for the conference to provide $50,000 to match each $50,000 raised by the trustees. Even before the proposed conference challenge could be adopted, the plan was amended to challenge the preachers of the Conference to subscribe $15,000 for a prayer room at the new Student Center. This proposal was initiated by Bill Hattaway, who as a minister was one of the most active of the trustees in moving the building program forward.

Eddy Scurlock was deeply moved by and appreciative of the generous role that the ministers were preparing to play, and although he still had some outstanding pledge balance on his women's dormitory pledge, he responded by making an additional pledge of $25,000 if the building starts "as soon as possible." Scurlock's generosity was matched by a $25,000 pledge from Walter Fair; $25,000 from Paul Pewitt; and "at least $10,000 for the same purpose" from Jimmie Owen. Latimer Murfee and Madison Farnsworth both pledged their support for the project, and Murfee moved that construction of the student center and dining hall begin "forthwith," as soon as finances can be arranged. Arranging of finances consisted of little more than going to see Tyler banker W.A. Pounds and carrying word of the pledges of trustees like Eddy Scurlock, Walter Fair, Paul Pewitt, Jimmie Owen, Latimer Murfee, Madison Farnsworth, and others. Board meetings had come a long way since the May morning in 1953 when Cecil Peeples had sat on the steps of Marvin Methodist Church in Tyler. They were now a source of exhilaration, an opportunity for recharging of the batteries, and an exercise in the expression of optimism and encouragement that were Peeples' natural state of being.

Poor health was taking a major toll on the life and service of H.F. Banker, and in April 1959 Banker submitted his resignation as a board member, thus ending his highly effective role as chairman of the building committee. Eddy Scurlock and Madison Farnsworth acted quickly to see that Banker was made an honorary life member of the Board. Tyler banker Abe Pounds was named to the building committee, and Eddy Scurlock was elected chairman of the committee.

As the decade of the 1950s came to an end the momentum of the building program was accelerating. The building fund note at Tyler Bank and Trust Company generally ran a balance of about $300 thousand, only because the commitments of trustees to new building efforts came just a bit faster than the actual payment of their pledges and gifts. Eddy Scurlock said in one of the meetings during this period that "I can stay out of debt in running my business, but I have a hard time keeping up with my pledges to Lon Morris College and to my church." Scurlock had been a charter member of Houston's Saint Luke's Methodist Church in the 1940s, and his involvement with Lon Morris had been cultivated at least in part by Durwood Fleming, Saint Luke's founding senior pastor. Scurlock enjoyed telling the story of how he came home from a building committee meeting at Saint Luke's one evening in the post-World War II years, and shared with Mrs. Scurlock the news that he had made a commitment that they would pay for the air conditioning system in the Saint Luke's sanctuary. She was described as thrilled and very supportive. Scurlock, probably embellishing the story a bit, went on to tell how he came home the next day and found a highly respected Houston contractor stationed outside his River Oaks home about to begin an air conditioning project.

As completion of the E.C. Scurlock Student Center was accomplished in 1959, the board's sights were set on further expansion of the college plant. The new facility was officially named "Scurlock Center" in honor of Eddy C. and Elizabeth Scurlock during the course of the first board meeting held there on April 27, 1959.

In a November meeting in 1959, Scurlock announced a $25,000 gift to be applied to a fund for building of a science

118

building, and his gift was matched by new commitments from Latimer Murfee and Paul Pewitt, each in the amount of $25,000 to be applied to science, library, and office facilities. Eddy Scurlock, together with Latimer Murfee, called for a start to construction of "a library, science building and office building as soon as physically possible." The razing of the Twin Towers was not a topic of much open discussion by the board, but it was clear that the building committee, at least, had heard and was heeding the S.W. Ray recommendation. It was interesting that planning talk was moving from the arena of the "financially possible" to the "physically possible."

The commitments of Scurlock, Pewitt, Fair, Murfee, and others made possible the start of construction on a science building in early 1960, and although the discussion of tearing down the Twin Towers was still a few months away, it was apparent that the placement of the science building pointed to a campus layout that did not include the Twin Towers as its centerpiece.

Along with the construction of buildings such as Scurlock Center, the Paul Pewitt Science Building, and new library and administrative facilities, there was building on another front. Improvements in faculty housing were critical to the attracting and retaining of quality faculty members. Fringe benefits including housing and meals were still necessary components of faculty compensation as the decade of the 1950s ended and the 1960s began.

Much building was done in the housing area between 1957 and 1962, and one of the movers and shakers in faculty housing was Arnold L. Reed, a Lon Morris ex-student of the pre-Peeples era who had achieved considerable success in the life insurance business in Little Rock, Arkansas, and who in the mid-1950s moved to Dallas and founded Great Commonwealth Life Insurance Company. Reed was a man with impressive sales ability, a big heart, and a genuine interest in Lon Morris College.

The meeting of Reed and Cecil Peeples happened sometime in the mid-1930s, not long after Peeples came to Lon Morris. Peeples was out making college contacts somewhere in Rusk County when he picked up a young hitchhiker who had been visiting in Panola County with a young lady named Nelva, who would eventually become Nelva Reed. Arnold Reed was on his way home to Alto. Peeples and Reed began an acquaintance that day that would flourish and continue up to the time of Reed's death in the early 1970s. They remained fast friends, and Arnold Reed's efforts in provision of better faculty housing were complementary to the larger building program being waged by Scurlock, his building committee, and the other trustees.

Reed had attracted positive notice among board members, even while still in Arkansas, when he advanced the idea for a "living endowment" program aimed at encouraging businesses and individuals to "put Lon Morris on their monthly payrolls." Arnold Reed set a shining example of participation in the early 1950s when he made a commitment of $500 monthly to Lon Morris support. It was also Reed's interest in marketing and personnel development that led to the creation of the Board of Development. This group, organized in the late 1950s proved to be a fertile training ground for trustee leadership, and was another of Arnold Reed's significant contributions to Lon Morris.

The building effort was boosted significantly and somewhat unexpectedly at a meeting held in Scurlock Center on

October 24, 1960. Peeples and Scurlock had been working quietly behind the scenes for months to secure a major building gift through the Simon Henderson family of Keltys. Peeples had available a building program brochure that looked to replacement of the Twin Towers with a new administrative and academic complex. After reviewing the need for the development of an academic center, Peeples introduced Simon Henderson, one of the newest members of the board, who announced that his mother and his family would like to provide the full cost of developing a new library facility. Board Chairman T.E. Acker, stunned but deeply moved and appreciative, called on Rev. John Wesley Hardt for a prayer of thanksgiving. This October meeting in 1960 was the first attended by Bishop Paul Martin, recently assigned as Resident Bishop of the Texas Conference. It was fitting that he be introduced to the Lon Morris board in one of its finest hours.

Eddy Scurlock proceeded to ask about the status of building fund finances, following which Cecil Peeples responded by distribution of a thorough and carefully prepared packet of printed reports. The board was on a roll, an all time high, but it wasn't quite ready to adjourn!

Jimmie Owen, formerly from Overton but now living in Lafayette, Louisiana, requested an opportunity to make a statement, and he spoke concerning the building program and his long association with several Lon Morris board members. He concluded his remarks in a surprising and dramatic fashion by announcing the gift of the new administration building.

As the commitment to building a new academic center sank in, there was swift action to raze the Twin Towers and to make way for the Simon and Louise Henderson Library and the Jimmie Owen Administration Building. In November,

1960, the Twin Towers building was torn down, and for a period of well over a year the administrative offices of the college were located in the residence on Prather Street that had once been the dean's residence.

The Henderson Library and the Owen Administration Building were the last of the buildings built by Arthur Thompson, but over a period of almost nine years, Thompson engaged in a very productive effort with the trustees and Cecil Peeples that saw the construction of every building from the Fine Arts Building to and including the construction of the new administration building.

Beginning in 1961 and continuing for the next three years, every Lon Morris board meeting became a forum for discussion and promotion of the campaign of United Capital Funds for Texas Methodist Higher Education, Inc. The campaign, a joint project of the five Methodist colleges in Texas, was calculated to raise some $32,000,000 for the institutions participating. The executive director and principal spokesperson for the campaign was Charles W. Musgrove, who became a regular participant on the agenda of Lon Morris board meetings for the course of the campaign. The Lon Morris portion of the campaign goal was approximately $3,520,000, or eleven percent of the $32,000,000 total.

The first board meeting in the Paul Pewitt Science Building was on November 1, 1961, a time during which the construction of the new library and administration buildings was underway.

As construction of the Henderson Library and Owen Administration Building began in 1961, the financing of the building program received an immediate and welcome boost. The Henderson family foundation was reimbursing library construction costs on a monthly basis. In practice the college received a check from the Henderson Foundation prior to the tenth of each month, just in time for the payment of the previous month's building expenses. Very little, if any, new debt was created in connection with library construction, and if there were any, it was a matter of short-term cash flow management.

In the case of the Owen Administration Building the construction costs outpaced payments for a few months, but even then Owen paid regularly at the rate of $2,000 monthly for more than a year, and then paid the balance of his building pledge in a lump sum shortly after completion of the building.

Eddy Scurlock's increased involvement in college financial affairs was the prime factor in moving most board meetings from Jacksonville to Houston during the 1960s and 1970s. Trustees like Scurlock, Madison Farnsworth, Latimer Murfee, Herb Dishman, Simon Henderson, Jimmie Owen, R.E. "Bob" Smith, and others found Houston to be the preferred site for quick and productive meetings. Peeples was happy to go anywhere Eddy Scurlock wanted to schedule a meeting because it was a certainly that Scurlock never wanted to meet without the expectation of some positive outcome. When the board met in Houston, it was usually at either the Houston Club, the Petroleum Club, or at Houston's First United Methodist Church.

With the completion of the library and administration building during the 1962-1963 school year, the building and construction emphasis changed from fundraising for buildings already built or under construction to planning for the next major facility to come. The citizens of Jacksonville had been actively pursuing the raising of building funds for a new gymnasium. The Lon Morris basketball program had been consistently successful for two decades, and had achieved national prominence under the leadership of coaches O.P. Adams, Marshall Brown, and Leon Black. The gymnasium in use at that time was the 1920s vintage frame building originally known as "Kiwanis Gym" and later simply as "Bearcat Gym" or the "Lon Morris Gym."

At a board meeting in September, 1962, the board noted the fundraising successes of the citizens of Jacksonville, and commended the local citizens for the raising of some $80,000 for new gymnasium construction. Cecil Peeples had expected that his board would appreciate and respond to this show of local interest and effort. At this same meeting in 1962, Eddy Scurlock gave the gymnasium project a great boost when he announced that he would pay $100,000 immediately on the outstanding balance of his pledge in order to reduce the building debt and to expedite new construction.

In April of 1963 the board was advised by Charles Musgrove of the United Capital Funds Campaign that Lon Morris had received approximately $100,000 net of its share of campaign expenses as its portion of "undesignated gifts" that had come in. This encouraging report prompted board action to authorize the seeking of bids for new gymnasium construction as soon as plans could be finalized.

The social, business, and financial circles in which Eddy Scurlock moved and lived created opportunity to challenge friends and business associates to support his interest in Lon Morris College and other philanthropic efforts. At one point in the 1960s Scurlock was in New York on a business trip when there was a highly publicized blackout, a general power failure of Consolidated Edison electric service through Manhattan and much of the Northeast. A few days following the incident, Cecil Peeples was in Scurlock's Houston office and was handed a $20,000 check from Leon Hess, a New Yorker and personal friend of Eddy Scurlock. Scurlock told Peeples with a broad display of his trademark grin, "I was on an elevator with Leon during the blackout last week, and since we were stuck there for about forty-five minutes I just decided to do a little work for Lon Morris." He just didn't miss many opportunities.

One of Peeples' goals that would bear good fruit after considerable tedious nurturing was the involvement of R.E. "Bob" Smith in the Lon Morris building program. Peeples and Scurlock, with the help of Charles L. Allen, worked diligently to get Smith to visit the Lon Morris campus, and eventually the visit was accomplished in the course of the United Capital Funds Campaign. As a part of Smith's role as general chairman of United Capital Funds, he made a commitment of $600,000 to the campaign. When his pledge was paid, it was allocated to the various colleges and universities according to the formula set out in the original campaign plan. The eleven percent that came to Lon Morris secured a place for Smith's name on the newly constructed "Vivian and Bob Smith Gymnasium" that was built in 1963 and 1964.

On October 25, 1963, the board, acting through the executive committee, awarded a contract for construction of the new gymnasium in the amount of $245,167. All of the construction up to this point had been done on a cost-plus basis with Arthur Thompson serving as the construction management liaison. The general contractor for the athletic facility was Clanahan Construction Company of Tyler, and the building was completed on schedule just prior to the start of the 1964-1965 school year.

At the time the gymnasium contract was awarded the board raised the college debt limit to $260,000. Essentially, this meant that all construction prior to the gymnasium had been paid for, and that the remaining debt after completion of the gymnasium would not exceed the bottom-line cost for that building alone. The plant expansion from the time of the A. Frank Smith Fine Arts Building through the Owen Administration Building would be paid-in-full. This was a significant accomplishment considering the fact that some thirteen residences for faculty and staff had been built or purchased during the same time frame when the larger building program was exploding.

Shortly after construction of the Vivian and Bob Smith gymnasium had begun, Eddy Scurlock surprised the board with an additional gift of land in Leon County, Texas, along with a contract to sell the property for a price that netted the college $50,000.

The construction of the Vivian and Bob Smith Gymnasium necessitated some additional street dedication, paving, and parking lot development in the area directly West of the A. Frank Smith Fine Arts Building and the library and administration complex. A link between Devereaux Street and Woodlawn Street was paved, with curb and gutter provided, concurrently with the gymnasium construction. The street was named to honor Madison Farnsworth.

By late February of 1964, with the gymnasium construction progressing on schedule, Eddy Scurlock began to press for building committee authority to begin construction of a boy's dormitory. When Eddy Scurlock began to talk about doing things "as soon as possible" he was providing a strong cue that it was time to begin. It was apparent that, as was the case in the building of the new gymnasium, the design and construction would be handled by architects and builders other than the long-used team of S.W. Ray and Arthur Thompson. The gymnasium had been designed by Burch and Bateman, Architects, of Tyler, but when it came time to design a new dormitory the board chose to work with Cates and Decker, Architects. By late September, 1964, the board was well into its working relationship with Jack Cates and Jack Decker, another Tyler firm that would design and supervise the next three buildings on the campus.

On December 15, 1964, the executive committee of the board met and awarded a construction contract to the Gary Arnett Construction Company for a price of $180,879.04, and the building of E.T. Clark Hall was underway. Dr. E.T. Clark was an uncle of Eddy Scurlock, and it had been Clark who, many years earlier, had loaned Scurlock some $5,000 that enabled his entry into the oil business. Eddy Scurlock's interest in the building program at Lon Morris was never in doubt on any project, but this particular one held a very special place in his heart. In the fall of 1965, fifty-six young men became the first residents of Clark Hall. In the summer of 1965, London Hall, which had served as one of the primary dormitories on campus since 1914, was torn down to make way for the next addition to the academic complex.

The summer of 1965 was the thirtieth anniversary of the Peeples presidency at Lon Morris. Except for the opening of Clark Hall as school began in the fall, the anniversary was largely unnoticed, but in Peeples' mind there were still goals

19. Gladys and Cecil Peeples stand in front of the Cecil E. Peeples Academic Center. (Mid-1960s)

to set and to be achieved. At this stage he was not talking about retirement, but it was later in 1965 that he first began to lay out a program that he wanted to see accomplished by the time of the college's one hundredth anniversary in 1973.

Good things were happening in the growth of endowment, and with Eddy Scurlock carrying the ball so often in the building area, Peeples felt freed up to increase his personal efforts in the securing and growing of endowment funds. The new campus was indeed emerging, but Cecil Peeples understood that a fine new building without a secure stream of future revenue for maintenance and operation was, in fact, a potential embarrassment waiting to happen. With that concern in mind he focused much of his energy on endowment emphasis.

At a meeting of the board at the Petroleum Club in Houston in December, 1965, Peeples called for a $3,000,000 campaign for the college's 1973 anniversary celebration. He targeted $300,000 for a women's dormitory, $500,000 to complete payment of costs incurred at Clark Hall and to provide future accommodations for approximately ninety men in either a second wing or in a separate men's dormitory. He called for $110,000 for modifications to present buildings plus an additional $40,000 commitment to the air conditioning of Fair Hall and the A. Frank Smith Fine Arts Building. The remainder, or almost 60 percent, of the $3,000,000 goal would be allocated to new endowment.

The board listened to the Peeples challenge with interest, and it was accepted with enthusiasm. Eddy Scurlock called for the immediate air conditioning of the Fine Arts Building and Fair Hall, saying that these were not really "long range" but that they should be completed prior to the start of the Summer session in 1966. And so it was. The board accepted the challenge, and the goals laid out would be realized.

The Higher Education Act of 1965 had just been passed, and there was a frank but very positive discussion of whether or not Lon Morris should participate in the Higher Education Facilities Act. The minutes of the board meeting that day record that:

Dr. Charles L. Allen spoke at length in favor of Lon Morris receiving federal aid and voiced the opinion that the institution could not long compete with state-supported institutions without such aid. Mr. R.A. Shepherd and Mr. E.C. Scurlock both spoke in favor of Lon Morris seeking federal help when the college had needs which it could not meet with its own resources. Madison Farnsworth raised the question of whether or not there was anyone present who was opposed to federal aid to higher education. There was no comment. Dr. Peeples suggested that the meeting should be recessed for lunch and that the remaining business of the day be transacted from the table after completion of the noon meal.

After lunch the meeting was resumed with a motion by R.A. Shepherd as follows:

RESOLVED that the administration of Lon Morris College be authorized to apply for and participate in any programs of federal aid to education, whether in the form of loans, grants, or by other means which might be deemed advisable by said administration and to which said Lon Morris College shall be entitled.

The motion was seconded by Mr. Farnsworth and carried unanimously.

In the Spring of 1966 the administration made application for a grant for a classroom building under the Higher Education Facilities Act of 1963. Notice of favorable action by the U.S. Office of Education and the Texas Coordinating Board for Higher Education was received in August of 1966, and a new classroom and teacher office building was built on Devereaux Street in much the same location from which London Hall had been removed a year earlier. The building contained eight general purpose classrooms, three classrooms for instruction in business administration, one classroom for instruction in art, one language laboratory, twelve faculty offices, one faculty workroom, one conference room, and related supporting facilities.

This classroom and faculty office facility would be the final building in the complex that became known as the Cecil E. Peeples Academic Center. The facility, built by Gary Arnett Construction Company, cost $235,886 excluding furnishings and equipment. The final development cost of the building was approximately $280,000 of which one-third was paid through a grant under the Higher Education Facilities Act of 1963. In late 1966 a building grant of $250,000 had been received from the Moody Foundation of Galveston, and the board proudly designated the building as the W.L. Moody Classroom Building. The grant from the Moody Foundation, together with the federal funds available, enabled completion of the building with no increase in the building fund debt, and no doubt accelerated the start of the next project that would be a men's dormitory.

The Moody Building was opened at the beginning of the 1967-1968 school year with a dedication ceremony including a full board meeting in Jacksonville on September 21,

1967. The ceremony that day took on special meaning for all Lon Morris supporters because it marked the first official function in which Cecil Peeples participated following his return from Houston after cancer surgery.

20. Cornerstone laying for Moody Hall Classroom Building took place September 21, 1967. Bishop Paul Martin wields the trowel. Also participating in the ceremony are E.C. Scurlock, member of the board and chair of the building committee, Tom Acker, chair of the board of trustees from 1937 to 1972, and President Cecil Peeples.

Even as the board celebrated the completion of the Moody Building, and viewed the challenge of building a new academic center as fully accomplished, Eddy Scurlock was calling for a new building project. He expressed the hope that it would be possible to have a new men's dormitory on the drawing board by early 1968. It had become something of a habit to conform to the building schedules that were suggested by Eddy Scurlock, and probably surprised none of the board that the plans for what would become Herman Brown Hall were developed during 1968. The construction of this men's dormitory was expedited by a $50,000 grant from the Brown Foundation of Houston.

Brown Hall was designed to house eighty-eight men, and was designed by Cates-Decker-Barber, Architects and Engineers. In January 1969, the board entered into a construction management contract with Gary Arnett with a negotiated management fee of the lesser of $12,000 or 4 percent of construction costs. The building was constructed between January and November of 1969 at a cost of about $300,000. The citizens of Jacksonville, and the Jacksonville business community conducted a campaign that targeted $60,000 as its share of the Brown Hall construction effort. The Brown Foundation had offered its $50,000 as a challenge grant, conditioned on the trustees raising $100,000 to apply to the effort. Barnes H. Broiles, publisher of the *Jacksonville Daily Progress* acted as general chairman of the local Capital Funds Campaign, and as the construction of the project got underway he attended a board meeting and reported that $46,927 had been raised, with significantly more expected when all corporate offices from outside Jacksonville were heard from. Once more, as in the building of the gymnasium five years earlier, Cecil Peeples and Eddy Scurlock expressed deep gratitude for the role that the Jacksonville community continued to play in the building effort.

Although Brown Hall would be the last building constructed during the Peeples presidency, provision for the next

133

major building was in place during the school year 1972-1973, the year of his retirement. In the spring of 1969 when it was evident that Brown Hall would be completed sometime that fall, Eddy Scurlock began to tout the desirability of planning and constructing another dormitory for women in the near future.

Peeples was planning his retirement to coincide with the school's one hundredth anniversary celebration in 1973, and from 1969 until he relinquished the reins to President John E. Fellers in June, 1973, his obsession became debt retirement, major gift cultivation, and endowment fund growth. Peeples had worked for years to cultivate the friendship, support, and long-term interest of Arthur R. and Evie Jo Wilson. Arthur Wilson was a retired Texaco executive, the son of a Methodist preacher, and a generous man in whom Cecil Peeples saw great potential. Wilson's wife, Evie Jo, was the daughter of a Methodist preacher who had also been highly successful as a businessman and investor. Evie Jo Wilson also possessed keen business skills and a generous spirit. The Wilsons' support of Lon Morris was significant well before Peeples' retirement, but during the final year of his presidency it resulted in the funding of what would become the Craven-Wilson Women's Building. The generosity of the Wilsons impacted not only Lon Morris but also several other Methodist educational institutions such as Southwestern University and Southern Methodist University. The dream of Craven-Wilson Women's Dormitory was fully realized with its completion in 1974, and Peeples' retirement was marked by the celebration and recognition of his long-term goal of a new physical plant "Debt Free in '73."

21.
**Gladys Peeples (Mrs.
C.E.), President Cecil E.
Peeples, Eddy C.
Scurlock, Elizabeth
Scurlock (Mrs. E.C.),
Jack Blanton Jr.,
Laura Lee Scurlock
Blanton (Mrs. Jack),
and Jack Blanton
in the early 1970s.**

135

22.
Debt Free
in '73
Celebration
in
Bob Smith
Gymnasium.

136

23.
Twin Towers
1909-1960

Courtesy of
Lon Morris College

24.
Lula Morris Hall
1925-1973

Courtesy of
Lon Morris College

25.
A. Frank Smith
Fine Arts Building
1954

139

26.
Fair Hall
1956

Courtesy of
Lon Morris College

27.
Scurlock Center
1958

Courtesy of
Lon Morris College

141

28.
Paul Pewitt
Science Building
1961

29.

**Jimmie Owen
Administration
Building.**

**C.E. Peeples
Academic Center**

**Simon and Louise
Henderson
Library**

1961

143

30.
Vivian and Bob
Smith
Gymnasium
1964

Courtesy of
Lon Morris College

144

31.
E.T. Clark Hall
1965

Courtesy of
Lon Morris College

32.
W.L. Moody
Hall
1967

Courtesy of
Lon Morris College

146

33.
Herman Brown
Hall
1969

Courtesy of
Lon Morris College

147

Chapter Eight

The Retirement Years 1973 – 1993 Building An Endowment
by
John Croft

In June of 1973, Cecil and Gladys Peeples opened a new chapter in their life. According to Gladys, Peeples had "no hobbies" in the usual sense, and she was a bit worried about what he would do with all his new-found spare time in retirement. Mrs. Peeples was looking forward to some extra time for study, travel, and housekeeping. She hadn't had much spare time during the Peeples presidency years. Reflecting recently on that period, Mrs. Peeples said that the retirement years were very happy ones for both of them.

On the third day of his retirement, Gladys Peeples knew things would work out for Peeples. He was an early riser, and she awoke to hear a typewriter clicking away. She knew that all was well and Peeples was going to be okay! He was launching a project that had always been a dream, but necessarily confined to the back burner during his college presidency. Peeples would write a book.

In his usual style, Dr. Peeples finished the book in record time. Its title, *A Whole Person In A Whole World*, says a lot about Cecil Peeples. It's a small book, about 70 pages, and a fine read. The book is dedicated to Mr. and Mrs. E.C. Scurlock. Dr. Peeples frequently referred to Mr. Scurlock as "the man of the century" insofar as Lon Morris College was concerned.

149

He also privately referred to Mr. Scurlock as his best friend. Several years earlier, Scurlock had encouraged Dr. Peeples to get immediate medical attention for a potentially serious ailment, and had seen that he received the best medical care possible. "He saved my life," Dr. Peeples once told a friend.

The book is divided into three parts. The first section " ... deals with the merging of the left and the right [politically speaking] in our world, our nation and our churches." Dr. Peeples advocated a balanced approach rather than the confrontational style rampant in America during the 1970s. He urged respect for heritage as well as recognition of the need for change.

In one part of the book, Dr. Peeples urged the "left" folks in the church and other organizations to be fair to the American form of government and economic system. He said:

> If you think our economic system is a thing of the past just remember that one little country of two hundred million people is feeding itself and helping to feed a billion communists as well as those in underdeveloped countries. This half of the truth is not brought out often by the networks or the national press. I have never heard of this being mentioned by a committee of social concerns.

In another section he also urged fairness toward the business community.

> I came to Lon Morris in 1935 with the attitude toward business men that is common today [1973-'74]. The college owed, in that bleak depression year

when students worked for fifteen cents an hour, approximately $30,000 in monthly bills, all overdue.
I sent each creditor [each month] a dollar and a half or maybe a little more to some on the larger accounts. To my utter amazement not one business man wrote an unkind sentence to me for faster payments. To my greater surprise many used a three-cent stamp to acknowledge the payment and write a note of encouragement.

On the other hand, Dr. Peeples urged the folks on the right to recognize the need for change in the present, not at some distant date.

... Changing conditions offer new opportunities to work toward the solution of some of our problems. From our best colleges and universities is flowing for the first time a sizable number of skilled, educated members of our minority groups. These young men and women must be allowed to go as far as training, talent and skills can carry them. This has not been possible in the past in either north or south. To do this will be good business, good patriotism and good Christianity.

The second part of the book dealt with a merger of the ideal with the practical at the personal level. Dr. Peeples was advocating a "wholeness" approach. He said:

... Worship can kindle and stir us to action ... Worship can lead to a destiny determining decision in one's life ... Worship can heighten and enrich fellowship ... Work can be a thrilling experience and an avenue toward wholeness ... We gain faith by recalling the past, hope by anticipating the future, and love by affirming the present ...

Part three contains a mini-biography of Dr. Peeples and family, a photograph of Dr. and Mrs. Peeples, some acknowledgments, and a statement by Dr. Peeples on the future of Lon Morris College, which he saw as bright indeed.

Dr. Peeples was a good writer, but he did much more during his retirement years. In 1973, he was now free to take on his second great mission for Lon Morris College. He was elected President Emeritus of the College, Life Member of the Board of Trustees, and Chairman of the Permanent Endowment Committee. In his eyes, the last office provided the opportunity for what he hoped would be his most enduring legacy to Lon Morris College. He was now able to work full time in building the endowment funds of the college. And build, he did! When Dr. Peeples came to Lon Morris College in 1935, it had a negligible endowment, if any. In 1973, the endowment stood at about $1,500,000. Through the efforts of Cecil Peeples, a number of dedicated trustees and friends of the college, and Divine Providence, the endowment exceeded $14,000,000 by mid-1993.

Gladys describes the Peeples approach to raising endowment funds as a kind of gentle persuasion. "He didn't ask for money; he just explained the need; he gave people the opportunity to help the college." He never looked down on small contributions or on small contributors. He encouraged the small givers who sometimes grew into major benefactors.

34. Cecil Peeples and Walter Harris are together during the 1981 Christmas season.

He appreciated every gift, every donor, and every donor's spouse. He would write lengthy, personal, somewhat chatty letters to prospective givers, – and similar thank you letters. Someone referred to one small gift as "peanuts"; but Dr. Peeples thought otherwise. He said, "If you put in enough peanuts, you get a good cash crop."

Peeples was able to encourage personal giving by the trustees better than anyone ever connected with the college. His touch was light, but it worked. His philosophy of trusteeship wasn't so much that every board member must contribute to the financial needs of the college, but that every member of the board must have good business judgment. If you are a part of the leadership, are able to help a worthy cause, and understand the needs, you will want to do your part. His approach was simple and effective.

During Peeples' retirement years, Belle Albritton was his able part-time assistant. She also worked in the business office. Mrs. Peeples describes Belle as "excellent; a great help." She kept the endowment records and helped with Peeples' heavy correspondence. Her files are full of correspondence with donors and prospective donors (pretty much defined as anybody ever connected with the college, the church, or the community). Belle has copies of letters to and from people of all walks of life. Peeples always contacted the leaders of companies or foundations whenever he wanted to tell the story of Lon Morris College. He knew that some could do more financially than others. It was Peeples' view that people at or near the top of a business organization were often "the lonely ones." He gave them his ear and a chance to do good for Lon Morris College.

Building the board was important to Cecil Peeples while he was president and afterward. Mrs. Peeples recalled some influential board members. Madison Farnsworth was impressed with the drama program of the college.

Farnsworth attended a Lon Morris drama department performance at his church and thought the actors were professionals. He became a trustee, and later brought Eddy Scurlock to the board. Mr. Scurlock's accomplishments in behalf of the college have been covered in another part of this book. Jimmie Owens heard the choir and was impressed with the college. Paul Pewitt, the largest single donor to the college, was a quiet but influential trustee. Lon Morris College received over $2,900,000 plus mineral interests yielding several thousand dollars a year from Mr. Pewitt's estate. Pewitt and Peeples enjoyed a common bond by having a Kentucky connection. Both had family there. They were personal friends

35. President Emeritus Peeples receives the Alexander Award given by the classes of '35, '36, and '37 at their 1985 reunion. Judge Morris Hassell presents the award, while Lon Morris President Faulk Landrum applauds.

as well as dedicated officials of the college.

In addition to book reviews for *The United Methodist Reporter*, Dr. Peeples represented his church and the college in numerous preaching and speaking engagements in his "retirement years." He was a great fan of George Washington. Washington represented the kind of patriotism and other values that Peeples most respected. Dr. Peeples would frequently speak about Washington or weave Washington and his values into his talks.

An outline of one of Peeples' speeches found in Belle

155

Courtesy of Gladys Peeples

36. Gerri Peeples Weddle, Gladys and Cecil Peeples, and Nelda Peeples Darrell are together in 1989.

Albritton's files bears the title, "Preserving Our Heritage In A Changing World." His handwritten notes all over the outline demonstrate that Dr. Peeples never finished a speech until it was delivered.

In this particular speech, Peeples remarked that Washington towered like a mighty peak over the Western Hemisphere, and was the greatest in a league of great men – Hamilton, Jefferson, Franklin, Madison, Marshall. Peeples made a very interesting comment to the effect that if Washington were living, he couldn't run on either the Democratic or Republican ticket. That statement might be even more profound than

Peeples intended.

While Peeples had a very active retirement during the first 20 years, his last two or three years were plagued with physical difficulties. He fell in 1992 and broke his hip. He never fully recovered. But he did his best to keep in good spirits and did what he could to encourage others to support the college.

About a year before his death, Peeples was named one of the distinguished alumni of his alma mater, Southern Methodist University. At the ceremony, the assembled crowd was called from the reception area to the auditorium by the triumphant sound of the SMU Trumpet Ensemble. Dr. Peeples and the other honorees were gathered on the stage of the Hughes-Trigg Student Center with representatives of SMU and the Alumni organization. Dr. Kenneth Pye, president of SMU, presided. Peeples and Pye had been friends since Pye became the president of the sister United Methodist institution. It was an emotional and thrilling time for the Peeples family and the host of friends and well-wishers present.

Cecil Edward Peeples completed his earthly mission in January of 1993. At his memorial service on January 22 at the First United Methodist Church of Jacksonville, Texas, the sanctuary was filled with United Methodist clergy and lay-persons; Lon Morris College trustees, administration, faculty, and alumni; and community leaders and friends. Gladys Peeples was a member of that church. Dr. Peeples had often preached there and was a regular worshipper, when he was in town. Their daughters, Nelda and Gerri, were brought up in that church – a special place in the hearts of the entire family.

Leading the service were three longtime friends of Cecil Peeples – Bishop John Wesley Hardt (retired), Dr. Don Benton of Dallas, and Dr. Asbury Lenox of Houston. They had been his students and he was very proud of the accomplishments of all three. Bishop Hardt's memorial sermon was entitled, "A Great Encourager." Dr. Benton read the scripture; and Dr. Lenox gave the eulogy.

Cecil Edward Peeples had joined the saints resting from their labors. There is no doubt in the minds of his many friends that he wears the victor's crown of gold. He was a winner. Cecil Peeples remains in the hearts and memories of thousands whose lives were touched by this great and good man and by his beloved Lon Morris College.

Chapter Nine

A Great Encourager
by
John Wesley Hardt

With the remarkable life of Cecil Peeples stretching across each decade of the twentieth century, my personal association can be traced across seven of those decades. My first memory of this tall, physical giant came in my sophomore year in high school, only a year after he became president of Lon Morris College.

Dr. Peeples was stopping to visit pastors across the Texas Conference, inviting them to encourage students to consider coming to Lon Morris, when he visited with my father who was pastor in East Bernard, fifty miles southwest of Houston. As I listened to the conversation, he turned to me and said, "I hope you will begin thinking about coming to Lon Morris when you finish high school."

Two years later, when we moved within forty miles of Jacksonville, and I had, in fact, made plans to enroll at Lon Morris, I received a handwritten letter of welcome from the president of the college, Dr. Peeples, that I have treasured and that illustrates his gift for encouraging people of all ages and circumstances. This treasured letter in his own handwriting is dated July 25, 1938:

My dear John Wesley:

We will be happy to number you as one of our students next year. The College owes a great deal to its students and we are going to try to do the most for them. I hope you are able to finance admittance into the Public Speaking Class.

As a young preacher you will have a great opportunity to help us in building a truly Christian Campus. If you do not already have such a habit, have a time each day to read some good devotional literature. While you are in the dormitory learn to get along with people, be friendly to all and at the same time avoid compromising in any way the highest ideals of your home training.

While one is developing critical attitudes, one must not lose the habit of boosting. Catch the true and best Lon Morris spirit and help to build an even better spirit.

There is a religious service on the Campus conducted by students each Thursday evening. You will find this hour as profitable as any you will spend. I sincerely hope you will plan to attend them throughout the year. Inez Condrey of Nacogdoches, a preacher's daughter, is President. They have about sixty present each week.

You have a good home environment, far above the average. And I know of no good reason why you shouldn't really "go to town." Mr. Watt of Mineola was telling me some very fine things about you recently. Never forget that I am here to help you when I'm needed. I shall be praying that you shall be one of those dependable, fine-spirited young preachers with good habits of study.

We shall be looking forward to seeing you on September 6.

Most cordially yours,
C.E. Peeples

As a student, I never forgot the times he stopped me with some word of challenge or reminder of some area of my conduct that might be improved. One day he engaged me in such a conversation saying, "You are making progress, but you could be much more effective if you learned to smile more often."

When he discovered that more than a passing friendship might be developing between me and another student who was working in his office as a part-time secretary, his interest seemed to become even more direct and intimate – in fact, he encouraged us both to consider attending his Alma Mater, Southern Methodist University. Somehow I found a copy of the letter that he addressed to Dr. Umphrey Lee, the new president of S.M.U., dated May 13, 1940:

Dear Dr. Lee:

If you will give John Wesley Hardt, a Ministerial student, a proposition similar to the one you gave Walter Ewing, he will come to S.M.U.

He is one of the most promising ministerial students we have had here. He is a member of the scholarship fraternity, one of the best workers we have ever had.

This young man and the lady I wrote you about are the two students who are perhaps most deserving and capable in our graduating class. I sincerely hope that you will do everything within reason to get these two students in S.M.U. You will have done a grand day's work for the university, for these deserving students, and to the Cause to which we are dedicated.

Thanks,
C.E. Peeples

Then, he never missed a chance to tell me that Martha Carson was the best secretary he had ever had, and that she had enough sense to be President of the United States. I have often wondered what he might have been telling Martha, but apparently it was not enough to discourage her from finally agreeing to spend the rest of her life with me.

After leaving school, he encouraged me with a constant stream of letters, by inviting me back to speak in chapel or in commencement events, and by seeing that I was invited to become a member of the College Board of Trustees after being out of school only a decade.

His letters and conversations about my appointments are too intimate to share, but I never doubted that there was at least one person who had great confidence in me and dreams for my life.

The amazing thing is how many students and others were made to feel the same confidence and expectations for their lives. Although many letters were lost, my files contain between one hundred and two hundred letters that bear his signature, – and the theme of counsel and encouragement and plain advice can be traced in each one.

Toward the end of his life, friends organized a flood of letters to the S.M.U. Alumni Association urging that Cecil Peeples be selected as a recipient of the S.M.U. Distinguished Alumni Award. This recognition was given, and on an inspiring evening on March 7, 1992, this honor was celebrated. As Dr. Peeples greeted well-wishers from his wheelchair that night on the S.M.U. campus, he said "I'm on cloud nine tonight."

Across the years, a strange and persistent infection had settled in one of Dr. Peeples' feet, and eventually required surgery. While limiting his mobility, it was an inconvenience that could only leave another obstacle to overcome. Then a more serious internal problem required surgery to remove a malignant growth. Peeples credited the generous concern of his board chairman and intimate friend, Eddy Scurlock, with insisting on getting the medical attention of the doctors and staff of the Methodist Hospital in Houston that opened the way for a full and complete recovery.

Through all the years, he never lost the pastoral touch in his genuine concern for people. He made hospital calls and conducted funerals and wrote endless letters to persons going through times of bereavement or illness. And he preached in the largest and smallest congregations of the Texas Conference, from the Red River to the Gulf of Mexico. He was a pastor always in the midst of the struggles and challenging issues of the revolutionary changes that were brought in the middle and latter half of the twentieth century. Hundreds of pastors and thousands of lay people looked to him for leadership in seeking to make a faithful witness and informed and intelligent witness to the meaning of Christian discipleship in this changing and challenging culture. He found a unique and wide ministry in offering encouragement and challenge to multitudes of individuals who were inspired to develop their highest potential because of the friendship and nurture which had come to them through some relationship with Cecil Peeples.

One vivid illustration of the way dreams and pragmatic realities were blended in the life of President Peeples was his years of service as one of the Directors of the Fair Foundation of Tyler. Walter Fair was one of the pillars of the Lon Morris College Board of Trustees during the early years when

Peeples was beginning the transformation of the campus. The architect for those first building programs was S.W. Ray, who was a brother-in-law of Walter Fair. When an effort was made by some of the preachers on the Lon Morris Board to name a new president, it was Walter Fair who was credited with saying to Bishop A. Frank Smith, "I don't think we need a new president."

Such confidence and trust developed between Fair and Peeples that Peeples was invited to become a member of the Board of Directors of the Fair Foundation, and the relationship between Walter Fair and Cecil Peeples was continued following the death of Walter Fair between Peeples and Wilton Fair and James Fair, sons of Walter. Peeples continued as a director of the Fair Foundation until his death, and he celebrated the privilege of directing an annual gift from the Foundation to Lon Morris College, in addition to other decisions in which he shared as a director. His presence was a blessing and a source of encouragement to the Fairs and to many across East Texas.

In Jacksonville, he was actively involved in the Chamber of Commerce, a frequent speaker at civic and community events, and the spirit of encouragement was repeated until it became entirely natural and spontaneous.

As he had written to me only a few weeks before enrolling in Lon Morris: "... as one develops the critical mind, one must also cultivate the spirit of boosting." He practiced that and demonstrated a positive and optimistic outlook even in the midst of circumstances that for others would have been disheartening obstacles.

Within the second decade of his administration at Lon Morris, two completely different threats cast shadows that tested his spirit of hopeful encouragement.

He began in 1935, during the Great Depression, with seemingly hopeless indebtedness. After eight years, in 1943, he was able to celebrate being free of debt. While the wartime economy may have allowed the debt finally to be paid, the war years produced other obstacles that threatened the future of this small school. Any thought of new building was impossible. He must have grown weary of continual questions about how long it might be before Lon Morris would have to be closed.

In the second decade of the Peeples' Presidency, two different threats were potentially devastating. With growing confidence that, after all, Lon Morris College might have a brighter future than had been previously predicted, some pastors in the Texas Conference began to suggest that Peeples had done his job and the time had come for a new President. This sentiment reached its climax in the early fifties when a special meeting of the Board of Trustees was convened in Marvin Methodist Church in Tyler. Speculation had even advanced to the point of offering the name of a candidate for the President of Lon Morris.

Only second hand memories remain, since those who attended that meeting have now joined the Church Triumphant, but as the story was told, the morning was spent with the mood indicating that the change was predicted. As the meeting adjourned for lunch, Bishop A. Frank Smith privately sought the counsel of the greatly respected layman, Walter Fair. This dedicated and generous Tyler layman was a man of few words, but he left no doubt about his opposition to what he had heard during the morning. His response to Bishop Smith was "I don't think we need a change." When the Board reconvened in the afternoon, the tone of the meeting took an entirely different direction, and Cecil Peeples was given a vote of confidence and a new mandate. From that day on, the lay members of the Lon Morris Board of Trustees developed a new intensity and loyalty in support of the integrity and vision of Cecil Peeples.

The second threat developed gradually. Peeples had become the senior member of the Administrators of Methodist Colleges in Texas, and there was increasing speculation that the remarkable and steady leadership of Peeples at Lon Morris would bring his name into consideration for an invitation to serve some larger college. When a vacancy developed at McMurry in Abilene, or Texas Wesleyan in Fort Worth, or Southwestern in Georgetown, or Southern Methodist in Dallas, or Centenary in Shreveport, rumors would include Peeples' name among possible successors. I never knew how serious those threats may have been, but at least they became distractions. For Peeples, any momentary distraction was quickly cast aside, and the increasing passion for implementing a new vision for Lon Morris was moving again.

During the fifties, the first new building in a generation became a reality, and then one building followed another. It was from the vision and continuing encouragement that Peeples was able to inspire the Trustees and benefactors of Lon Morris to follow the leadership which was creating a new campus and promising future for this historic school.

With former Lon Morris students now assuming increased leadership in congregations of the Texas Conference, support developed for recognizing his leadership on a wider basis, and so in the election of delegates for the 1948 meeting of the South Central Jurisdictional Conference of the United Meth-

166

odist Church, Cecil Peeples was among those chosen to represent the Texas Conference.

In time, he became the Senior Member of the Association of Presidents of Methodist Colleges in Texas. While the recognition of his leadership reached across Texas and beyond, his positive and optimistic spirit was recognized and often utilized in a variety of ways by the citizens of Jacksonville, where he had become one of its most widely known residents. A frequent speaker at Rotary or Lions Clubs, he also served as president of the Chamber of Commerce. Civic groups and schools across East Texas called upon him for inspiration and counsel, so that with his continuing appearance in United Methodist churches of the area, his striking appearance was recognized and his inspiring encouragement left its mark in hundreds of places among thousands of people.

When the time for retirement came, nearly four decades had passed, and a completely new campus had been created. It was the encouragement and inspiration which Cecil Peeples had passed on to a Board of Trustees, to a Faculty, to an Annual Conference, and to one generation of students after another that had produced one miracle after another, and which had left the image of The Great Encourager as the picture of Cecil Peeples which multiplied thousands of women and men had indelibly imprinted upon their memories.

The style of this characteristic spirit of stimulating encouragement may be illustrated from another example from the many letters which he wrote. The following letter was dated January 18, 1982, and addressed to me in Oklahoma City:

Dear John:

The result of your influence and devotion to Lon Morris grows. I'm sure you recall raising some funds to start an endowment in memory of Mr. C.W. Conn, Sr. His son, C.W., Jr., is now a very valuable trustee. He has increased this endowment to fifteen thousand dollars. His address is: P.O. Box 2538, Beaumont, Texas 77704. How about writing him a note commending him for this great work he is doing for Lon Morris?

The $3,500,000 from the Paul Pewitt will starts flowing into the endowment February 1. You first got Mr. Pewitt interested in Lon Morris and got me a date to visit with him. Much later, A.D. Lemons talked to him about including Lon Morris in his will. No one was more excited about your election to the episcopacy than A. D. He is now in his nineties, living at 120 High Street, Henderson, Texas 75652. If you would drop him a line letting him know I told you about his getting Lon Morris in the Pewitt will, he would treasure that letter as long as he lives. All retired people, except me, get lonely.

The endowment is now over four million. Thanks again.

C.E. Peeples, Chairman
Permanent Endowment Committee

A similar letter dated five years later illustrates his enthusiastic and creative excitement for the Endowment Fund. This letter is dated June 9, 1987:

168

Dear John Wesley and Martha:

Enclosed is a receipt for your gift to the Zula Pearson Endowment Fund. We are very grateful to you.

How did you do it? John, you ran a college dairy, a very time consuming job, and Martha, you did half of my work and a third of Mrs. Pearson's, and yet both of you came out with top grades.

How do you do it? You gave the endowment fund a house, got burned out twice, serve a state that has faced disaster from the fall of oil prices and flooding, and yet you remember a great teacher.

To say you are an inspiration to us is the understatement of the year. One hundred thanks.

> C.E. Peeples, Chairman
> Permanent Endowment Committee
> and President Emeritus.

Only a year after receiving the Distinguished Alumni Award from SMU, as his physical presence had come to an end, a host of friends and citizens from across the state gathered with his family in First United Methodist Church, Jacksonville, to celebrate his life and recall personal memories of "The Great Encourager."

Three former students who had continued lifelong and increasingly intimate association with Cecil Peeples were privileged to join the pastor, Matt Idom, in leading the service. Don Benton compared his life to a tree described in Psalm 1. Asbury Lenox gave the Eulogy that is included later in this book. I chose the biblical story of Barnabas, who was remembered as "A Son of Encouragement," to recall many expressions of challenge and encouragement that had endeared

169

him to so many people.

If institutions are the lengthened shadows of individuals who have given their energy and resources to develop those organized and continuing values among human beings, then the gift of encouragement must be one of the priceless treasures that the Creator has allowed human beings to share. Surely multiplied thousands of women and men will strive and dream for Eternity with the great expectation of sharing that Eternal Vision with the Great Encourager, Cecil Edward Peeples.

Epilogue
by
Don Benton

*Blessed is the man who walks not in the council of
the ungodly, nor sits in the seat of the scornful, nor
stands in the way of sinners; he shall be like a tree
planted by streams of water. Whatever he does will
prosper and his leaf will not wither ...*

Psalm 1

The psalmist must have known a man like Cecil Peeples.
Cecil Peeples stood straight and tall like a tree. His roots ran
deep in the soil of truth in Jesus Christ fed by the springs of
living water of the Holy Spirit. His confidence for life was in
the God who had blessed him. He also believed that God had
gifted him to be a blessing to many, especially to young people
at the critical stage of choosing a direction for their lives.

Like a tree, many of us leaned against the trunk of this
tree we called "Dr. Peeples." He was solid to the core. He did
not waver nor bend too far regardless of the winds of change
and circumstance. He was a steady and reliable strength. We
who leaned on him found that we could be supported to stand
tall and erect when we stood with him.

Like a tree, the life of Cecil Peeples had many and long
branches. His thought always was on how those branches
could benefit and give shade and produce to the life of the
people of Lon Morris College.

Dr. Peeples' branches reached out to people who could
share his dream of a quality of life and of education for every
aspiring student who wanted to begin his higher education at
Lon Morris College.

To his family, he was a strength upon whom they could rely as husband and father. His dreams were shared by them as well.

To the many benefactors of Lon Morris, Cecil Peeples was not just another fund raiser, he was a friend who gave them an opportunity to be participants in an important service to humanity by helping to shape its future.

To faculty and staff, Cecil Peeples was a man they knew they could trust. Often at lesser salaries than they might have received elsewhere, they chose to serve with this leader and to share his vision.

Of course, none have felt more blessed than the students who had the privilege of standing in the shadow of this man, and to gather the fruits of his wisdom and of his labors. We know we also have been blessed. What Cecil Peeples has done has and will continue to prosper. The fruits of his labors will not perish, because of the love and gratitude in which he will always be remembered with high esteem.

When I graduated from high school, my future, I thought, was very uncertain. No one in my family had been to college so I had no encouragement to go. We also had no money to pay my way.

In July of that summer, God changed that. I was called to preach. My pastor suggested that I visit Lon Morris College. I had not ever heard of Lon Morris before then. We went to visit. When I met Dr. Peeples, he assured me that with a scholarship and working on campus, I could attend Lon Morris. So I enrolled. With the scholarship aid and the jobs I was given, my parents did not have to pay anything for me to begin my higher education.

I had several jobs on campus, – in the kitchen, the dormitory, basketball manager, and bus driver of the old '49. My favorite job was being chauffeur to Dr. Peeples. We made many trips together and became good friends. I learned much from his wisdom and encouragement.

The Lord certainly knew I needed a tree. He planted Cecil Peeples right where I needed him to be at a critical moment in my life. After graduation from Lon Morris, Dr. Peeples continued to follow my life so as to encourage me in growth and development. I owe much to him for who he was and where he was at a pivotal point in my life and my calling. I will always be grateful.

Eulogy

Dr. Cecil E. Peeples
August 5, 1902 – January 20, 1993

Delivered by Asbury Lenox on January 22, 1993
First United Methodist Church, Jacksonville, Texas

We are gathered today to celebrate the life, leadership. and ministry of Dr. Cecil E. Peeples. He was a distinguished citizen, an outstanding educator, a marvelous teacher, an ideal role model, a tireless traveler, a successful fund raiser, an enthusiastic civic leader. He was a devoted husband, a loving father, and a super grandfather.

Some institutions are but the lengthening shadow of an individual. Certainly Lon Morris College is the lengthening shadow of Dr. Cecil E. Peeples. He came to be president of the college in 1935. It was the middle of the Depression, and times were tough. The future of the school was uncertain. Some said that Dr. Peeples was sent to Jacksonville to preside over the demise of Lon Morris College. Instead, he presided over a resurrection of the college, and it has been growing strong and stronger for more than five decades.

The story of his life is the story of a "Ministry of Recruitment." First, he began to recruit students. He recruited many full-paying students. He recruited many students who were deserving but needed a little assistance. To help provide an education for those with some need, he recruited donors of scholarships. Then, he would match together the donors of the scholarships and the recipients in such a constructive way

175

that both could feel very positive.

Good trustees are a requirement for the support of an institution. Dr. Peeples had a marvelous manner and ability to recruit strong and effective trustees. His style was such that as the trustees served, they learned to love God more deeply, to love the church more enthusiastically, and to love Lon Morris College with generous hearts.

His timing and uncanny ability to recruit faculty was a key to the successful educational experience provided for the students. He shared a magnanimous and nurturing spirit which blessed the faculty and had a trickle-down impact upon the whole student body.

Furthermore, Dr. Peeples recruited donors of buildings, and across three decades there were ten new buildings and resources provided for an eleventh one. He was so successful in building a new school plant that, when we came in 1973 to the celebration of the Centennial, the college had a complete new plant and was debt free.

Most of you know that upon Dr. Peeples' retirement, the Board of Trustees named him President Emeritus of the College, a life member of the Board of Trustees, and Chairman of the Permanent Endowment Fund Committee. To increase the Permanent Endowment Fund became, for him, a crusade. It was his belief that the security and future of an institution was predicated upon a substantial endowment fund. With zeal, he made visits, phone calls, and wrote letters asking everybody everywhere to set up and contribute regularly to a permanent endowment fund account. His efforts were marked with enormous success.

Knowing him . . . as you know him and as I know him . . . it would not surprise many today to think that he has already contacted Peter, James, and John and asked them to set up a permanent endowment fund account at Lon Morris College. Dr. Chappell Temple, if you receive an anonymous gift within the next ten days to the Permanent Endowment Fund, it just might be heaven sent.

Dr. Peeples, dear friend . . .

You came in a century when we needed you;
    you blessed and strengthened an institution;
    you blessed and strengthened every one of us;
    and thousands of others . . .

You taught us how to love;
    you taught us how to live;
    you taught us how to serve;
    you taught us how to give.

You will always be a part of our lives. As long as we live, we will continue to love you and to thank God for you.

Amen

Dr. C.E. Peeples

Born August 5, 1902, Lingleville, Texas
Died January 20, 1993, Jacksonville, Texas

Survivors
Wife, Mrs. Gladys Peeples
Daughters and Son-in-law, Nelda Darrell of Owensboro,
Kentucky; and Geraldine and Vernon Weddle
of Los Angeles, California
Brother, Vance Peeples of Los Angeles, California
Six Grandchildren: Richard Weddle, Bobby Darrell,
Kirk Weddle, Bart Darrell, Bracken Darrell,
and Shelley Chatfield
Four Great-Grandchildren: Drew Darrell, Aaron Darrell,
Anderson Darrell, and Joshua Weddle
Several Nieces and Nephews

Pallbearers
Walter Harris, Norris Starkey, Grady Singletary,
Wilbur Phifer, A.G. Acker, Rev. Virgil Matthews

Honorary Pallbearers
Dr. C. Chappell Temple,
Members of Lon Morris College Administration and Faculty,
and Ministers of the United Methodist Church

Final Resting Place
Resthaven Memorial Park, Jacksonville, Texas

(Information from the funeral order of worship)

Selected Writings
of
Cecil Peeples

Building
Texas Methodist Higher Education
Through the United Capital Funds Campaign
by
C.E. Peeples
Lon Morris College
Written in the early 1960s

I want to bring you face to face with one of the most decisive issues before America today. It is simply this: Will we keep our dual system of higher education? That is, will we have colleges supported by both the state and the church, or will all of higher education drift under the domination of the state? There is no tension between church colleges and tax-supported schools. My thesis is we need both, but can lose one.

In early America all colleges were church and private schools. In 1952 for the first time there were more students in tax-supported schools than in church and private colleges. At the present time 60 per cent of the students are in tax-supported schools. It is estimated that by 1970 seventy per cent of our boys and girls will be in colleges owned and operated by our government. The rapid sweep toward statism can be illustrated in this way: The University of California (that's far enough away to be safe) secures an annual appropriation for operating expenses exceeding the endowment income of the thirty most highly endowed universities in America, and that includes such institutions as Harvard, Columbia, Yale, and Rice University.

Another amazing fact is that philanthropy in recent years is shifting from church colleges to schools owned and operated by the government.

On the national scene there are just two churches in higher education in a big way. One is the Roman Catholic Church with 266 institutions, and The Methodist Church with 136.

Let me gorge you now with enough facts about Methodist Higher Education to cause intellectual indigestion. We ought to take great pride in our Methodist higher education system, which includes the following great universities:

Southern Methodist University, Dallas
Emory University, Atlanta, Ga.
Duke University at Durham, North Carolina
American University, Washington, D.C.
Drew University, Madison, N.J.
Boston University in New England
Syracuse University in New York
Northwestern University, Chicago, and
The University of Denver in the West.

Also, we have many of the very finest four-year colleges and twenty-one robust, growing junior colleges.

Coming closer home, there are five Methodist institutions of higher education that are sharing in the United Capital Funds Campaign, along with the Wesley Foundations. In 1938 our general Board of Education made a state-wide survey of our colleges. They reported that we had more schools than we were supporting. They recommended that the schools best located to served the church be kept and strengthened, and the remainder be closed. We did just that. During the last few decades we closed Clarendon College at Clarendon, Wesley College at Greenville, Kidd-Key College at Sherman, and we gave away the University of San Antonio. The remaining carefully selected institutions are well located to serve our church effectively. Southern Methodist University is in an excellent location to serve the South Central Jurisdiction. The other colleges are as follows:

Texas Wesleyan College at Fort Worth in North Texas,
McMurry College at Abilene in West Texas,
Southwestern University at Georgetown in South Texas, and
Lon Morris College at Jacksonville in East Texas.

Let me insert here an urgent plea for the support of our Wesley Foundations. Two of the most promising Methodist ministers of my acquaintance attended Lon Morris College. I suppose each of them talked to me at least a half dozen times about becoming a preacher. After graduating with us they attended The University of Texas, and while working in the Wesley Foundation there, found their way into the Methodist ministry. I would like to stress with all my strength that you support the Wesley Foundations.

But why maintain church colleges, you ask? In the first place, we do not want all of higher education under one agency, whether it be The Methodist Church, the Roman Catholic Church, or the government. If you have been in a land where all of higher education is under one agency, you know the tragic results. It is still true that absolute power tends to corrupt and dominate. Look at what happened to Germany in Hitler's day. See what is happening in Russia at this moment, and realize that human nature is the same in Berlin, Moscow, Jacksonville, Houston, and Washington. Absolute power corrupts and dominates absolutely!

In the second place, it is cheaper to keep our church colleges. Across the country students attending state institutions pay 20 per cent of their way. Students attending church colleges pay 32 per cent of their way. General Robert Smith, a great business man in Dallas, said that while it is impossible to estimate with complete accuracy, as best he can figure, it takes $2.40 to send a tax dollar to Washington and return it to the counter of The University of Texas.

In the third place, over 80 per cent of our preachers are products of church colleges, as are many of our choice laymen and laywoman. Remember this—it is not the purpose of our tax-supported schools, or of the Roman Catholic church colleges, to train the Methodist Church a leadership. If we have such a leadership, in the main, we must train it ourselves.

The United Capital Funds Campaign is an effort to raise $32,000,000.00 for our Methodist institutions and Wesley Foundations for two purposes only—building and endowment.

I do not have to tell you that modern, functional, sanitary, and well-equipped buildings are essential. When people lived in log houses the college might be defined as Mark Hopkins on one end of a log and a student on another, but your children coming out of modern homes are not going to sit on a log and get an education, and you are not going to send them there.

The need for adequate endowment is becoming an obsession with me. There is no other way to give to our institutions strength, stability, and the power to secure and hold capable and exciting teachers. College inspectors are nice intelligent people, but at least one of them will have ice water for blood, and a good endowment income will help to thaw him out. As long as I am at Lon Morris College the Endowment will increase each month. If someone else doesn't give to the endowment fund, I will place part of my gift there.

And now a word to you laymen:

First, support your local church budget. In it are many exciting causes–it's the life stream of our church.

Second, if you would fling your influence across our land, support regularly, monthly if possible, at least one educational institution of the church. Why not share in preserving our dual system of higher education and in the training of our young preachers and laymen?

Now may I say a word to my preacher friends – supporting this program wholeheartedly and enthusiastically will help your local church budget. I hope I would have enough faith to say this if I were a pastor. Just look around the state and you will observe that those who are building our Methodist colleges and our Wesley Foundations are the leading donors to their local church budget. We preachers have more at stake in this than anyone else. Once all of higher education is under one agency, the free pulpit is gone.

Now our problem is simply this: While the dollar per member program is one of the greatest things that ever happened to our church colleges, and while the few individuals who have supported our colleges and Wesley Foundations have been most generous, only an amazingly small percentage of Methodists have ever written a personal check to a Methodist college or a Wesley Foundation. We are vitally interested in the number of contributions as well as in the amount given. Although our schools and Wesley Foundations need the most generous gift you are in a position to make over a period of five years, it should be remembered that enough small gifts are like the many small swollen streams which cause the river to overflow.

If we neglect our church colleges and go to Washington every time we need money for higher education, we will go down into Egypt some day for this intellectual food and not return. The whole tide is away from church colleges and the stream is swifter than you realize. Will you also go away? A dead minnow can float down stream. Our plea is for great laymen who will swim against the tide and who will accelerate the speed with which we strengthen our colleges and our Wesley Foundations. If we do this, we will lead our people toward freedom, toward the church, and toward God.

Lon Morris College History
by
C.E. Peeples
Written in 1986

There are three ways to enjoy life: recall the past, live in the present, and anticipate the future. A college that doesn't reverence its past, doesn't have a future. Over a century ago Dr. Isaac Alexander, a great pioneer educator and religious leader, had a date with destiny when he founded, in Kilgore, Texas, Alexander Collegiate Institute, now Lon Morris College.

Although Dr. Alexander was a strict disciplinarian, as were most teachers in that day, he was a highly respected teacher and Christian leader. In those distant days, their world was very different from ours. The boys sat on one side of the classroom and the girls on the other, with a partition coming up to the teachers desk separating them. Rules were very rigid. Students caught smoking were summarily expelled; those who survived, and many did not, were equipped to face life and lead in building a great civilization in East Texas

It is no exaggeration to say that Dr. Alexander's former students idolized his memory. He was a dynamic leader and in great demand as a speaker. We realize that moral education is impossible without an habitual vision of greatness. In an age that has lost its heroes, the memory of our stalwart founder challenges us. Even now, decades after he was hushed in breathless sleep, his spirit is enshrined in the hearts of Lon Morris students. Even yet, every decade or two, they revive the old historic school song:

Alexander, Alexander
Alexander, Alexander
We will never cease to love thee
Alexander, hail to thee.

We recall, with gratitude those who survived the great depression of the 1930s, one of the most trying periods in Lon Morris history. Soup lines were long. Students worked on public projects for ten and fifteen cents an hour. Some married couples in school at that time were actually hungry and had too much pride to let the world know they did not have sufficient food. Loyal faculty members worked overtime with very little pay to keep open the doors of Lon Morris College. They and their families ate in the college dining hall because they could not buy groceries. Perhaps John Bunyan described the mood and determination of this college generation:

The hill, though high, I covet to ascend
The difficulty will not me offend
For I perceive the way to life lies here.

Through it all Lon Morris survived.

The great depression was brought to an end by another world tragedy, the second World War. During the long history of Lon Morris, our school survived two bloody world struggles and other disturbances called "brush fires." The second World War is more vivid in our memories. A megalomaniac, Adolph Hitler, brutally suppressed all traces of democracy in Germany and converted his land into one deadly military machine. He taught race superiority and brutally slaughtered six million innocent men, women, and children because they were of another race. Hitler sent his legions across Belgium, Denmark, the Netherlands, and France, and tried to bomb Great Britain into submission. At the same time the War Lords of Japan made a sneak attack on Pearl Harbor on Sunday morning, December 7, destroying most of the American navy. This act of infamy plunged an indignant America into global conflict. Congress declared war on Germany, Italy, and Japan.

Patriotic young Americans rushed off to join the Army, Navy, Marines, or Air Corps. Others were drafted into service. Howard Martin, the Lon Morris Business Manager, said, "Everybody is talking about the war and doing little about it." He resigned, joined the Navy, and was soon in charge of a boat in the Southwest Pacific. While on duty he spotted the periscope of an enemy sub, dropped a depth bomb and destroyed it before it could sink his vessel. Millions of Americans were escorted across the waters by naval vessels to England, Africa, and Southeast Asia.

As the months dragged on, the tragedies of war struck home. Messengers were busy delivering messages, "We regret to inform you"; wives lost their husbands, children were orphaned, young ladies said, "Good-bye" to their sweethearts only to learn later they would never return. Billy Gene Martin, President of the Student Association, joined the Air Corps. Later he flew his big bomber over the campus, tipped his wing and disappeared into the wild blue yonder. While on a mission over northern Germany, his plane received a direct hit and disintegrated. Years later we went to the Central Baptist Church in Livingston, Texas, and laid his remains to rest. We watched his parents grieve their way into premature graves.

Although we realize that war unsettles everything and permanently settles nothing, the most avowed pacifist will agree that these young men saved us from the tyranny of a mad maniac. Their supreme sacrifice challenges us and their memory haunts us in the quietness of the night and disturbs like the music of pain and joy.

How did the college keep its doors open during this long, destructive upheaval? An able, resourceful young teacher started a civil aviation school sponsored by the Secretary of Commerce, Jesse Jones. When war was declared, the college made a contract with Wallace Phillips, a licensed pilot, to give both ground and flight training to a Naval Aviation Training School that had been awarded to Lon Morris College. This flying school kept the school from closing. Civilian enrollment had decreased to sixty girls and seventeen boys.

The young Naval Aviation Cadets met classes in the old Twin Towers Building and made their initial flights from a small airfield where Nichols-Kusan is now located.

As one class finished its initial training, another came. The air was filled with naval aviation cadets. Two or three of these fellows did a little hedge hopping and landed their planes in trees. They escaped with cracked skulls, but throughout the history of the school there was not a single fatal crash. Some of these young flyers made names for themselves. James Parker was with General Doolittle when he bombed Japan. C.L. Newburn was shot down over water but was rescued. Joe Donaldson's plane landed in an Alaskan snowbank where he stayed for in interminable time with a broken leg. His experience was featured in the Saturday Evening Post.

Mr. Phillips divided his profits with the college and again Lon Morris survived one of its darkest hours.

Most of the years in Lon Morris history were delightful and remarkably carefree. Occasionally, there were instances of almost unbelievable dedication and achievement. For about two decades the junior colleges of Texas had state one-act plays and choir contests. Competing with about twenty entries, the one act play cast, directed by Mrs. Arch Pearson, and the choir under the direction of Miss Thelma Martensen, almost without exception, brought back first place trophies.

In one drama contest the leading role was played by a Jacksonville student, Betty Ray. The day before the contest, Betty went to the hospital with a strep throat. Another Jacksonville girl was assigned to the .part. She and Mrs. Pearson rehearsed until three o'clock the next morning, drove to Hillsboro for the finals, and that young lady was named best actress in the state. She is now Virginia Beall Ball of Muncie, Indiana, one of the top benefactors of Lon Morris College. In another contest, another Lon Morris student who had only one brief scene with only a few lines was named best actress. That young lady, Ruth Alexander, now heads the Drama Department at the college.

The dedication, the united drive of these students as they prepared for these contests defied description. Their director challenged, encouraged, drove, and inspired them on to perfection. One year, as they left for Hillsboro Junior College, the president of Lon Morris told them that if they won first place to call him collect, and if they didn't win first not to call. The evening rolled by and the 'phone didn't ring. Oh well, he thought, we can't win them all, and retired. In the early hours of the morning he was awakened by the noise of many voices. Lights from the cars caused him to fear that the main building was on fire. The front door had a large glass pane. As he approached it he saw through the glass pane, a large first place trophy. The cast, stage hands, and light crew were all yelling at once, celebrating! They didn't go to Hillsboro to get honorable mention, or to get second place; they went to be NUMBER ONE, and they had a trophy to prove it! The record of this drama club continues. Some thirty ex-students have appeared on the New York stage, on TV, or in movies. Programs have been given before national audiences in Nashville, Tennessee, Cleveland, Ohio, and Purdue and Kansas Universities. Choir units have performed in Atlantic City, Mexico City, Chicago Stadium, and Madison Square Garden.

Lon Morris has had some memorable days in sports. Carl Reynolds, from Bullard, played all the sports. He went on to Southwestern University back when that school played, and often defeated, the best university teams in the state. After graduating he played professional baseball with the Chicago White Sox and took part in one World Series. He was voted into the Texas Athletic Hall of Fame.

Until football became too expensive for private junior colleges, Lon Morris fielded a team. In 1935 Coach Puny Wilson signed up a Jacksonville High School graduate, Phil Moseley. Phil's father was a great athlete and was voted a member of the Baylor University Athletic Hall of Fame. Phil was a Phi Theta Kappa Scholarship student, played quarterback on the football team and was captain-elect for the 1936 season. That season he visited a relative in Wichita Falls, dived off a board only three feet above the water, hit the water at the wrong angle, and broke his neck. The bone specialist, Dr. Carroll, from Dallas was summoned. He told Phil that if he tried to set his neck there were nine chances out of ten he would not survive. If he didn't try Phil would be paralyzed from the neck down for the rest of his life. Phil told him to set his neck. When he did, Phil passed away.

We spoke at his memorial service in the Central Baptist Church where Phil had been active in youth work. When school started that Fall, a memorial service was held in the old Twin Towers auditorium. Coach Wilson did not want this young man to be forgotten. We heard him tell the squad that Fall that he hoped, when his young daughters grew up, they would marry young men like Phil.

In his freshman year Phil had played his best game against Kilgore. So the coach and team decided to dedicate that game each year to Phil's memory. The Moseley tradition carried on when Coaches Arch Pearson and Wallace Phillips were at the helm.

While the rest of the country was in the grip of the great depression, Kilgore was experiencing an oil boom. It was the only school that could finance a good football program. In the Spring players would go over to Kilgore and try out. If they couldn't make the squad, they would come on to Jacksonville and play for Lon Morris. Our boys, trying to win one for Phil, and also trying to convince the Kilgore coaching staff that they couldn't judge talent, worked all season to get ready for the Kilgore game.

The student body caught the spirit. Harold Brown, a good organist, in the week before the Kilgore game, would go up to the auditorium, open the windows, and play tunes that had been played at Phil's memorial service. The usually noisy campus was unusually quiet that week. Lon Morris had been losing games by forty points, and Kilgore had been defeating the same teams by fifty points. But when Lon Morris played

Kilgore, odds went out the window.

That year the squad worked on a trick play all season to be used against Kilgore. We traveled to Kilgore for the game. The coach persuaded the college president who played on an undefeated junior college team, to sit on the bench with them. He agreed, but determined to preserve his presidential bearing. Late in the game, with the state champions seven points ahead, a member of the squad said to the president, "Look out, this is the first of a series of three plays and the third is the trick play." The first two plays were designed to get the defense looking in the wrong direction. When the third play was called and our little guard, Johnny Petrash, who ended up carrying the ball, ran through a befuddled defense, the stands were going wild. A Lon Morris tackle dumped the safety and Johnny crossed the goal line. What was the college president doing? He completely forgot his dignity and was standing on the players' bench, waving his top coat over his head and yelling to the top of his voice.

Lon Morris has done well in basketball, going to the Nationals twice. Who can ever forget O.P. Adams and his lightning quick Puerto Ricans, who could jump higher and run faster than their taller opponents; nor can we forget Leon Black's boys playing Kilgore in the Jacksonville High Gym when Jim Bob Smith dribbled the length of the court in the last seconds of the game and scored the basket that sent Lon Morris to the Nationals.

Lon Morris graduates have shown up in places of leadership far out of proportion to their numbers. From the Science Department came Dr. Joe Walker, rated by many as the top anesthesiologist in Texas. John Wayne Croft, another Jacksonville native, is one of the top lawyers for Exxon. Many are business leaders in many fields.

Although only a small proportion of Lon Morris students are members of the life service organization, graduates of the school occupy many responsible positions in the church. At one time seven of the eleven United Methodist District Superintendents in the Texas Conference were Lon Morris exes. President Faulk Landrum came out of Mineola to Lon Morris. Jack Hooper, another Jacksonville boy, is pastor of Alamo Heights, San Antonio, the largest church in the Southwest Texas Conference. Dr. Don Benton, who drove the college bus to get through school, is now pastor of the third largest United Methodist Church in the world, Lovers Lane in Dallas. Bishop John Wesley Hardt, who presides over the Oklahoma Area, worked in the College Dairy to make his way through school. If president Landrum were to visit every church whose pastor is a Lon Morris "ex" it would require three years of his time.

The influence of the college has extended beyond the borders of our nation. Ruth Jones went to Africa a missionary, and was secretary for the bishop. Later Maude Reed began her missionary work on the same continent. At an annual conference session, they were assigned as room-mates. There they met for the first time. Late one evening one of them mentioned Lon Morris. The startled young ladies realized they were both graduates of the Twin Towers institution. After reliving their days here, at the hour of midnight, deep in the heart of Africa, they lustily sang the Lon Morris school song.

An institution that does not look to the future will get run over by the future. The future of Lon Morris holds possibilities far beyond the dreams of its most imaginative forebears. Operating in a modern, functional, debt-free plant, the college board of trustees is in a successful drive for ten million endowment, easily the largest philanthropic effort in the history of the school. As this endowment increases good teachers will be held and other great teachers will be attracted. Already the endowment has grown to $4,322,000, and that much more is in sight.

In the future the college will assist more teachers in further study, attract outstanding teachers and students, and become recognized as one of the top academic institutions of its kind. Students leaving our campus in the decades ahead will continue to be singing:

> In our hearts we'll ne'er forget thee
> Alma Mater fair,
> But eternal love within them
> For thee we will bear.

> Morris, Morris, dear Lon Morris
> Surely thou wilt be
> Ever worthy of our homage;
> Morris, hail to thee.

Book Reviews
by
C.E. Peeples, President Emeritus
Lon Morris College, Jacksonville, Texas

During his retirement years, President Emeritus C.E. Peeples wrote more than twenty-five book reviews for *The United Methodist Reporter*, reaching people far beyond those who had known him as president of Lon Morris College. The following are a few of those reviews, reprinted through the courtesy of *The United Methodist Reporter* and Mrs. Gladys Peeples.

***

Preaching The Good News
By George E. Sweazey
Prentice-Hall, Inc.
339 pp.

Preaching The Good News just may be one of the best books on preaching. The author covers every phase of preaching. If a mother of eleven children cannot choose a favorite, the grateful reader will have difficulty choosing a favorite of the thirty-eight chapters: A review could be written about each.

The author quotes Aristotle, Shakespeare, Phillips Brooks, Mark Twain, and the man in the congregation, yet every page is a reflection of the personality of a great scholar who served a pulpit Sunday after Sunday. What an unforgettable way he has of saying things! He mentions a sermon that "begins nowhere, goes nowhere, and leaves nothing behind." "Never talk down to your audience; they are not there." "When a preacher thinks, 'I am going to ring the bell today,' that is the day no bells rings." He quotes a rural pastor on the need for a wholesome environment, "If you put a pig in the parlor, it isn't the pig that gets changed." A minister must apply a Christian truth to an actual human situation, otherwise "a biblical sermon may get no closer to where we live than Palestine, and two thousand years ago."

There are enough ideas in two chapters, "Examples of Sermon Structure" and "Words," for a lifetime of study and growth in effective preaching. When I started preaching, an older minister said to me, "When a preacher goes in one hole and the congregation knows where he is coming out, it is time for him to move." The author gives in one chapter twenty different examples of sermon structure. In the chapter on effective words, he reminds us that Jesus never talked about "humanity," but spoke of "your brothers." He gives many examples of words to favor and words to avoid. These chapters are a diamond field for any minister who desires to explore more effective ways to a pulpit ministry.

One cannot afford to miss his chapter on "Style." "Style is a safer index to character than the face." A slipshod style is an accurate reflection of a slipshod character.

He appreciates the great and sometimes enlarges their contributions. Quoting Phillips Brooks, "'Preaching is truth through personality,'" he adds, "in the midst of personalities." This bears out recent surveys that indicate a prayerful, expectant congregation may be the most decisive factor in an effective preaching service.

This book is written for laymen as well as ministers, in a clear, arresting, and interesting style. Reminding us that a sermon must move from a problem to a procedure and action, he simply illustrates by saying that one man moving down the aisle of the church attracts attention because what is moving is noticed.

It is an inexhaustible book; the more you dig the more pay dirt you find. If I were forced to choose one book on preaching, I would enthusiastically select *Preaching The Good News*. It will be great news for any congregation when their pastor reads and uses it.

***

Prayer In World Religions
By Denise Lardner Carmody and John Tully Carmody
Orbis Books, Maryknoll, New York, 1990
168 pp.

In an age when what happens in one country may affect economically and politically the whole world, what more appropriate volume than one on "Prayer in World Religions."

The authors state that they have assumed a Christian audience and do not treat Christian prayer. They do treat six groups: Judaism, Islam, Hinduism, Buddhism, Native American religions, and African religions.

Dialogue among the world religions is now necessary and a certainty, they indicate.

The book is readable, but it is not for the superficial reader. It is a treasure for the average reader and the best minds who have not made a specific study of this field.

Space permits mentioning only a few significant features. The concluding chapter, "The Worldwide Imperative to

Pray," is one of the most profound chapters this writer has read. It belongs to the ages.

A brief survey of world religions makes clear the omnipresence of prayer.

Prayers of petition, thanksgiving, adoration and sacrifice are world-wide and fill the minds and hearts of people the world over. Divine grace is the favor extended to human beings in making it the gift of human fulfillment.

***

Bringing Out The Best In People
By Alan Loy McGinnis
Augsburg Publishing House, Minneapolis, Minnesota
191 pp.

McGinnis believes helping other people grow can be life's greatest joy.

Every paragraph in *Bringing Out The Best In People* relates to this one goal; and yet he realizes that any virtue carried to the extreme becomes vicious, that there is a simple solution to every complex problem and it is always wrong.

A superficial reader might feel the book is full of contradictions and inconsistencies.

The author tells of one man who wasted his life and influence and was overburdened with a sense of guilt. As a young man, he considered the ministry and didn't preach.

In another instance, he tells how guilt may lead to a better life.

He believes the positive is better than the negative approach, but not always. He believes that we must listen to people in need, and yet he tells of the superintendent of a small Sunday School with nine teachers, including the pastor, asking for five minutes the next Sunday morning. He rightfully diagnosed their hopes and needs, reminding them that they wanted better opportunities for their children. He said the members of the Sunday School didn't feel they knew enough to teach but added you will learn more in six months of teaching than you will in six years of listening. He gained 21 new teachers, and the church later became a large one.

McGinnis is a strong believer in the church: "One person against many is seldom a match."

He also tells of a man who failed for a time because he made too many positive statements. This man didn't spend enough time questioning and listening to people. He changed, and his only purpose became helping others recognize what they wanted and helping them to decide how to get it. In dealing with individuals, he questioned until that person suggested some goal to which he could relate and then helped him/her realize it.

McGinnis abhors the idea of planting some idea in the mind of people and making them believe it was their idea. That is manipulation and will backfire. He says he has yet to find a person who didn't have some worthwhile goal that he could encourage.

The author suggests 12 principles or rules to guide us in motivating ourselves and others. The book is filled with exciting and stimulating ideas, ranging from building inner drive to establishing high standards of excellence.

He stresses the power of example. His success stories include business, political, or religious leaders.

He tells the story of Harry and Ada Mae Day. Harry

planned to go to Stanford, but his father's death forced him to take over a ranch of 270 square miles. The Days moved into a four-room adobe hut without modern conveniences in the middle of the ranch.

After Sandra was born, her mother taught her at home. She grew up, went to Stanford, and later Mr. and Mrs. Day saw Sandra Day O'Connor take the oath of office as the first woman on the Supreme Court of the United States.

Beneath all these apparent inconsistencies is a dominant faith.

Whether you are a parent, executive, teacher, minister or friend, you can gain satisfaction that comes from "Bringing Out the Best in People." It is the most helpful book of this kind that this reviewer has read.

***

Clinging, The Experience Of Prayer
By Emilie Griffin
Harper and Row, Publishers
72 pp.

On the very first page of this volume, the author leaves us in a state of shock. The first three sentences must be quoted:

> There is a moment between intending to pray and actually praying that is as dark and silent as any moment in our lives. It is the split second between thinking about prayer and really praying. For some of us this split second may last for decades.

We approach this split second under cover of being too busy, having family objections, or even serving God in other ways. "We think we are praying all the time and we are not."

Dr. Ralph Sockman reminded us that Christ is the door into the sheepfold of prayer, dreaming and planning, and also the door to the pastures of work, service, and worthwhile achievement. The author of this volume deals only with what happens in the sheepfold of prayer, where spiritual imagination may be focused and kindled.

She reminds us of the oft-quoted verse, "They that wait on the Lord shall renew their strength." One version translates this verse, "They that give in to the Lord ..." Naturally, the author faces a paradox of life with a chapter on "Yielding" to God. All life is built on paradoxes and contradictions. We gain love only by giving it away and we become benefactors of mankind only by losing our life in service. Until we are totally committed and seek first the Kingdom of God, the secondary and necessary things will not be added. Prayer helps us get our priorities in order.

The author does not evade the difficult question, namely how to pray. It is difficult to set aside times each day to prepare for prayer and to pray. Yet all of us spend many minutes each day, she adds, in conversation with people who certainly do not care for us as God does. What the saints didn't tell us was that God's love is so close by, that reaching Him is as simple as turning one's face to the Lord instead of to the wall.

Emilie Griffin believes prayer is a very personal matter. For each of us the way lies straight ahead. We are all unique. "What the Lord is asking me, He is asking no one else."

The best reason we pray is that God is there. The by-products of prayer are many. God gives us assurance and confidence and awakens our sense of destiny. How amazing it is to love and be loved! To find such a spiritual friend is to be found and to discover our own sense of identity. Prayer gives us a growing clarity that results in love, joy, peace, patience, understanding, and faith and, above all, the sense of wonder that God is with us.

The author has saturated her life in the scriptures and quotes many great devotional passages of sacred writ. She has a profound insight into the literature on prayer and knowledge of it and gives a bibliography at the end.

Clinging is a small book of 72 pages. It is beautifully bound. In addition to being a valuable addition to one's library, it would be a beautiful gift to a friend. This writer has found it very arresting, stimulating and helpful.

***

The Kingdom Within, Revised Edition
By John A. Sanford
Harper and Row, San Francisco
188 pp.

It may be no exaggeration to say that if Bible readers in general and pastors and church school teachers in particular will read *The Kingdom Within* thoughtfully, our church will re-discover the individual in a fuller and a very impressive way.

In addition, it will receive many new insights into the meanings of Jesus' sayings.

John Sanford, a psychotherapist, applies the principles of depth psychology to the teachings of Jesus. The chapter that he rewrote in revising the book may be the most arresting chapter in the book.

He writes: "The soul today is an orphan. Philosophy, her father, long ago decided she did not exist and cast her aside. The church, her mother, fell unwittingly into the clutches of an extroverted, rationalistic materialism of our times and so also abandoned the soul; she did not notice that is losing the soul, she lost her ability to relate the individual to God."

Mr. Sanford states that humans always have known they have enemies. However, we may not realize that we carry within ourselves an inner adversary.

There is a Prodigal Son within each of us who carries us into a "far country" where we may be driven by wrong or secondary priorities. There's also an Elder Brother who may tempt us to be ungrateful, unforgiving and jealous. The adversaries within us, unless resolved, create evil, Sanford writes.

Also helpful is his application of depth psychology to each of the "hard sayings" of Jesus. "If any man comes to me without hating his father, mother, wife, children, brothers, sisters, his own life too, he cannot be my disciple" (Luke 14:25-26).

Of course, Jesus loved his mother. One of the last things he did was to ask John to take care of her. But when Mary and his brothers realized his teachings were getting him into trouble and wanted him to return home, he refused.

What he actually hated was the tendency to let peer or home influence deter him from realizing his own unique talent and purpose in life.

Although Jesus taught that narrow is the way that leads to life and sacrifices are necessary, he never leaves us facing a locked door.

We are challenged to go on toward wholeness, completeness and toward the development of our unique talents. That will lead to worthwhile social commitment.

***

There Is Still Love
By Malachi Martin
Ballentine Books, New York
199 pp.

Malachi Martin is an imaginative and interesting writer. His approach is all his own. He tells five parables based on true stories.

A disillusioned prostitute was redirected by a visit from Mary of Magdala.

A married couple that seemed to have a perfect marriage drifted apart until a "Grand Canyon" separated them. Bible characters, Aquila and Priscilla, pointed the way to bridge the chasm.

A promising college student thought, why not try everything, and ended up in a suicide attempt. He then met the disciple John and learned the meaning of love.

A man whose family was a recipient of part of a well-run, prosperous company was horrified when his nephew merged it with a cut-throat one that laid off trusted employees. The enraged man remembered that Jesus suffered a greater betrayal.

Finally, a minister of a church that had grown under his long pastorate was moved to a larger neighborhood church named John the Baptist. The preacher was failing and finally realized he was failing because he was preaching to please a worldly congregation. He changed and began preaching like John the Baptist of old and gradually brought the members back to church.

Author Martin apparently makes no distinction between the historical Jesus and the Risen Christ. He dismisses the idea of preaching the social gospel or preaching on any issue that might have a political connotation.

However, if you feel lonely in God's world, feel that what you do doesn't matter, think that our complex society is growing more impersonal and is gradually changing your name to a statistic, and wish a more personal faith, this book is for you. The author has an unshaken conviction that there is still love and that God's love can change your life.

Malachi Martin is a fascinating writer. The book is so interestingly written that your greatest difficulty will be to stop before you have finished reading the entire book.

***

Contemporary Growth Therapies
By Howard Clinebell
Abingdon, 1981
303 pp.

Howard Clinebell's *Contemporary Growth Therapies* is perhaps the most helpful book this writer has read. It condenses in uncluttered fashion an invaluable library in one volume. Where else can one get such clear insight into the contributions and limitations of Freud, Adler, Rank, Fromm, Horney, Sullivan, Frankl, Jung, Rogers, Rollo May, and others?

The second half of the book deals with effective group therapy procedures. It is written in an interesting and readable style.

This is not a book for the uncritical reader. One or two of the above were atheists and another was a communist sympathizer. But each has something to contribute toward our knowledge of growth therapy, and some of them had deep religious insights.

The volume has two distinct values. It points to the rich potential in each of us, how to put "arms and legs" on our plans, and how to use these resources for continuous growth. Also, these therapists point out ways we use our talents to cope with and contribute to society. One states that there is no purely individual act. If a man is sitting alone on a creek bank fishing, he is thinking about whom he is going to tell about his big catch.

Another psychiatrist points out how to escape the "tyranny of oughts and shoulds," and to use those creative ideas and goals that "Energize" us. In pulpit language, it is how to move from duty to Christian privilege, which after all is what the New Testament is all about.

The conscientious reader of this book will learn how to overcome those "dream-squelching" attitudes and obstacles that block personal development, and discover surprising avenues for continuous growth. There is much here for persons who want to continue to grow whether they be young, active, or retired. Don't miss it!

The School Songs

Alexander

Alma Mater

Music arranged by Jane Nelms

Words by E. M. Stanton

From the land of the blue bonnets, Al - ma Ma-ter
Mid the pine hills of East Tex- as in old Cher- o-
In our hearts we'll ne'er for- get thee, Al - ma Ma-ter

dear,___ all thy no - ble sons and daugh-ters
kee___ sweet - est mem - o - ries will clus - ter,
fair;___ but e - ter - nal love with - in them

bid thee joy and cheer.
mem - o - ries of thee. Mor - ris, Mor - ris, dear Lon
for thee we will bear.

Mor - ris, sure - ly thou wilt be___

ev - er wor - thy of our hom- age; Mor - ris, hail to thee.

211

Toward the 21st Century

37. Cecil Peeples helps great-grandson Joshua Weddle keep his balance on the Lon Morris College campus. And countless numbers of students, before this day and still to come, are keeping their balance because of the influence of Cecil Peeples.

Index

Boger, R.G. 31
Bradley, (Rev.) 43
Broiles, Barnes H. 98, 107, 133
Brown, Harold 193
Brown, J.E. 110
Brown, Marshall 61, 124
Bryan, Dawson 110, 113
Buckner, R.C. 64
Bunyan, John 188
Burton, (Coach) 9
Burton, Richard E. 68
Butler, F.E. 31
Buttrick, George 19

C

Campbell, T.D. 86
Cannon, Neal 87
Carroll, (Dr.) 192
Carson, Martha 162
Cashman, John 51
Cates, Jack 127
Chambers, Dunbar 110, 113
Clark, E.T. 127
Clendenin, Stewart 87, 113
Condrey, Inez 160
Condrey, Valerie 72
Conerly, W.W. 52
Conn, C.W., Sr. 168
Cook, Joe B. 97, 100
Cope, Burney 53
Craig, Bill xiii, 7

Flinn, Glenn 35, 41, 85
Ford, John W. 100
Fordyce, Helen 60
Fordyce, Robert 59
Fort, Homer 110, 113
Fosdick, Harry Emerson 19

G

Gilpin, Robert 87
Goodloe, W. Robert 12
Goodwin, W. Glenn 88, 110
Gould, Jay 24

H

Hairgrove, O.P. 67
Hall, Sallie 27
Hallonquist, Grady 52
Hardt, John Wesley iii, xvi, xx, xxiii, 53, 71, 116, 121, 157, 159, 161, 195
Harris, Finis 65
Harris, Frances Beall xvi, 65
Harris, Walter L. iii, xv, xvi, xxi, 49, 66, 83, 97, 103
Hassell, Morris xv, xix
Haygood, Hooper 62
Heflin, James 87
Henderson, Simon W. 95, 98, 121, 123
Henderson, Simon W. and Louise 94, 121
Hess, Leon 125
Hitler, Adolph 188
Holman, W.W. 90
Hooper, Jack 195

Horner, Jerry 62
Horton, Johnny 62
Hotchkiss, Lena 95

I

Idom, Matt 169
Iguina, Manuel and Louis 63

J

Johnson, Lyndon B. 66
Johnson, Ronald 68
Jones, Glendell, Jr. 105
Jones, Jesse 43, 190
Jones, L.Q. 57
Jones, Ruth 195

K

Karow, Marty 64
Kelley, C.C. 100
Keyes, Roger 60
Kiely, Ed xvi, 60, 61, 92
Kirk, Laura Lou xiii, 2, 3
Kirk, Mary Ellen Pollock 2
Kirk, Robert 2
Kirk, Robert Alexander 1

L

Labenski, Gladys xiii, 7, 8, 9
Landrum, Faulk xv, 31, 195
Langham, Robert 87
Lee, Clifford 31

Lefler, M.L. 31
Lemons, A.D. 110, 113, 168
Lenox, Asbury xx, xxi, 53, 62, 158, 169, 175
Likens, Margaret 27
Lowe, Lee Ella 1

M

Marshall, Elbert and Jane xvi
Martensen, Thelma 59, 89, 191
Martin, Billy Gene 189
Martin, Howard 71, 189
Martin, Paul xiv, 96, 97, 121, 132
Martindale, Margo 57
Matthews, Virgil xvi, 66, 67, 97
McBroom, Amanda 57
McKenzie, Emmett 62
Molloy, C.D. 56
Molloy, Pearl 38, 56
Moody, Wayland 41
Moore, Arthur 100
Moore, George 103
Morgan, H.T. (Herman) 31, 83, 85
Morgan, J.J. xiii, 10
Morris, Lula 25, 28
Morris, R.A. (Lon) xiii, 25, 26, 27, 28, 35
Moseley, C.P. 62
Moseley, Phil 192
Murfee, Latimer 86, 97, 100, 117, 119, 123
Musgrove, Charles 96, 122, 124
Musick, Helen xvi

N

Newburn, C.L. 190
Nichols, Lewis W., Sr. 41, 87
Nichols, Robert L. 88
Nichols, Talley W. 88, 90
Nicholson, W.R. 86
Nunn, G.J. 31

O

Odom, Ernest 90
Odom, Wayne C. iii, xx, 33, 53
Ousley, Bo 64
Ousley, Pat 80
Owen, Jimmie 94, 95, 98, 99, 117, 121, 123, 154

P

Parker, James 190
Paschall, Celeste Cincinnati 1
Pearson, Arch 49, 53, 59, 61, 63, 103, 193
Pearson, George W. 100
Pearson, Zula 20, 39, 49, 57, 60, 74, 78, 169, 191
Pearson, Zula and Arch xvi
Peavey, Don 87
Peeples, Alfred H. 1
Peeples, Cecil E. xiii, xiv, xv (Because Cecil Peeples'
    name appears throughout this book, no attempt has
    been made to list all of the pages.)
Peeples, Cecil E. and Gladys vii, xiii, xiv, xv, 38, 48, 72,
    83, 128
Peeples, Clyde xiv, 47
Peeples, Gerri and Nelda 115

Peeples, Gladys iii, xiii, xiv, xvi, xx, 1, 33, 35, 41, 57, 135, 149

Peeples, Glenn xiv, 47

Peeples, Lois xiii, xiv, 4, 5, 47

Peeples, Nelda xiv

Peeples, Perry Lovick (Pete), Jr. xiii, xiv, 2, 3, 47

Peeples, Vance xiv, 47

Perry, Nancy 49, 55

Petrash, Johnny 78, 194

Pewitt, Paul 100, 117, 119, 154, 168

Phares, Gil 100

Phifer, Ernest 87

Phifer, Jeannie Mae 68

Phillips, Annie Laurie xvi

Phillips, Wallace 43, 53, 55, 57, 61, 93, 113, 190, 193

Pollock, Mary Ellen 1

Pounds, W.A. 95, 117

Pye, Kenneth 157

Q

no entries

R

Ragsdale, Homer and Lorene 91

Rameriz, Potota 64

Ray, Betty 191

Ray, S.W. 114, 119, 127, 164

Reaveley, Ruth 59

Reed, Arnold 95, 119, 120

Reed, Cecil 62

Reed, Maude 195

Reed, Nelva 120
Renta, Alberto 63
Reynolds, Carl 192
Riley, James Lee 53
Robinson, Henry V. 49, 50
Robinson, Maudine 51
Roosevelt, Franklin 89
Rounsaville, James H. 100

S

Sartain, A.Q. xiii, 10
Scales, Bill 53
Scurlock, Eddy Clark ix, xiv, 94, 95, 97, 98, 100, 110, 111, 114, 116, 117, 118, 119, 121, 123, 124, 126, 127, 129, 130, 132, 133, 135, 154, 163
Scurlock, Eddy Clark and Elizabeth 118
Scurlock, Elizabeth xiv, 135
Shamblin, J. Kenneth 97
Shattuck, Kate 58
Shepherd, R.A. 100, 130
Shotwell, I.T. 85, 87, 88
Shotwell, Mrs. I.T. 38
Sills, Lillian xxii
Slater, Eugene xiii, 10, 11
Smith, A. Frank 43, 92, 94, 109, 111, 164, 165
Smith, Donnella 49, 51
Smith, Jim Bob 194
Smith, R.E. (Bob) 96, 123, 125
Smith, Robert 184
Smith, Vivian and Bob 61, 125
Sparling, Jack 87

Stalen, (Dr.) 98
Stanton, E.M. 31, 36
Starkey, Norris 79
Stewart, W.E. 86, 110
Strother, W.K. 27, 29, 31, 103, 105
Summers, (Coach) 16
Swain, W.R. 110

T

Tapp, Jennie 27, 28
Temple, Chappell 31
Terry, R.C. 110
Thompson, Arthur 94, 111, 114, 122, 125, 127
Thornton, Frank xvi
Tower, Joe Z 110, 113
Tubbs, Billy 79
Tune, Tommy 57, 77
Turrentine, J.B. 31

U

no entries

V

Vance, Marvin 87

W

Walker, Jack 103
Walker, Joe 194
Walker, P.W. xiii, 7
Walters, Evelyn 89
Ward, Travis 100

X

no entries

Y

no entries

Z

no entries